FROM KINGSBRIDGE TO CANARSIE

Published by NY Writers Coalition Press,
a division of NY Writers Coalition Inc., Brooklyn, New York.
For orders and information please contact

NY Writers Coalition Inc.
80 Hanson Place, #603
Brooklyn, NY 11217
(718) 398-2883
info@nywriterscoalition.org
www.nywriterscoalition.org

ISBN 978-0-9787794-3-6

Printed and bound in Canada.

Library of Congress Control Number: 2008933730

BOOK & COVER DESIGN BY Sohrab Habibion/Shadowless Kick
COVER & AUTHOR PHOTOS BY Jason Gardner; EXCEPT Jennifer Arzu by Kesha Young
CHAPTER PHOTOS COURTESY OF EACH AUTHOR
SELECTED NOELLE TANNEN & FAITH HARRIS NEIGHBORHOOD PHOTOS BY Elissa Benes
TITLE FONT: Champion HTF Heavyweight
TEXT FONT: Adobe Garamond Pro

FROM KINGSBRIDGE TO CANARSIE

REFLECTIONS BY 8 NYC GIRLS

JENNIFER ARZU, MAKEDA GAILLARD-BENNETT, FAITH HARRIS,
SOFIJA KULIKAUSKAS, ALYSSA LA CAILLE, JULIANNE REYNOSO,
ZAIRA SIMONE, AND NOELLE TANNEN

EDITED BY KESHA YOUNG

» FOREWORD «

When I first heard about the premise of the Neighborhood Story Project, youth writing about life in their neighborhoods and documenting it through interviews and photographs, I was intrigued. Through my studies in cultural anthropology, I had been exposed to the idea of understanding the self through cultural lenses. With writing as a reflective practice, one can become aware of the ways in which one has been acculturated. Through noticing and recording events from daily life, details from environment and conversations with elders, parents, peers, and community members, the seemingly routine practices that make up our lives become a visible shape, a pattern that defines the unique placement of our lives.

This book brings together eight teenage girls from diverse ethnic backgrounds, economic statuses, and family structures to explore self, neighborhood, and coming of age in New York City. The combined practice of writing about themselves as members of their families and communities, as well as observers of their communities, makes for extraordinarily clear images of cultural identity. Issues addressed in their writing, interviews, and photography interconnect spheres of family, race, ethnicity, class, religion, education, gender, sexuality, environment, politics, the arts, and global dynamics. The reader experiences an essence of a culture, time, and place in **From**

Kingsbridge to Canarsie: Reflections by 8 NYC Girls.

The process of curating this project has brought many moments of awareness, and I am truly grateful for the support my family and friends have given me throughout. I have had the privilege of reading many stories, interviews, and reflections that have helped me gain a more thorough understanding of life in New York City. I have grown to appreciate the different ideas conveyed and questioned by these authors. Making choices about the most effective way to present the people, their images, and their conversations has yielded a collectively created cultural artifact that I am eager to share. I invite you to step into the worlds illuminated by these noteworthy young authors and to experience perspectives on New York that you can't procure anywhere else!

Kesha Young
NYC Neighborhood Story Project Director/Editor
August 2008

»INTRODUCTION«

The students at Urban Academy High School come from all over the city. With only 130 students in the school and 291 distinct neighborhoods in New York City[1] many travel to Urban every day as the sole representatives of their 'hoods. Whether or not they love their neighborhoods, they defend them as their homes. If they hear their communities described in terms of gentrification, poverty or violence, they invariably argue that the whole story isn't being told.

When we were approached by NY Writers Coalition to continue the work of the Neighborhood Story Project, we knew that our students would be eager to tell their own stories. We decided to teach a course on urban anthropology so students could read ethnographies of other places and observe and reflect on their own neighborhoods. Twenty students joined the course hoping to become the new, young voices of their neighborhoods, speaking out on issues of urban development and urban blight. As they wrote, however, their stories became more personal. They shared writing about their blocks, their daily walks to their subway stations, and their families' histories in their neighborhoods. They talked about the ways they wanted outsiders to see what they know so well.

---

1. according to the NYC Department of Planning

This fall eight of those students chose to continue writing with us—eight girls in different grades and different neighborhoods. They came to this project with more or less writing fluency and varying levels of experience in persevering through a project of this scope. They toured each other's neighborhoods and responded to each other's writing. Sometimes they were surprised at the differences between neighborhoods in the same borough, and sometimes they were surprised at the elements they saw repeated throughout the eight communities they represent. These stories are pieces of the puzzle of similarity and difference found in New York City told through the eyes of teenagers who have grown up here.

Caitlin Schlapp-Gitloff & Becky Walzer
Urban Academy High School Teachers

» OUR PATHS LED US ALL TO URBAN ACADEMY «

not so beautiful rose
JULIANNE REYNOSO

I started my high-school experience going to Theodore Roosevelt High School, or "Rose," in the Bronx. It was a big old building that was broken down into many other smaller schools. The school I attended on the Rose campus was Belmont Prep. I don't even know why I ended up there. It was a relatively new school and there weren't any statistics on the school. The only reason I even applied was because of my mother. She convinced me that it was such a cool school since they broke down the original TRHS to smaller schools, and she told me it had a pool.

When I found out that Belmont was the school I was going to, I was pretty mad. It made me wish that I had never listened to my mother and applied. I never wanted to be so close to home. My whole life I've been going to the neighborhood schools, and in high school I wanted to break free. I wanted a reason to come home later and I wanted to ride the train.

Being there was horrible; my first year I actually took my social studies class with Special Ed students. I remember being like, "WTF am I *doing* here." The only way I survived that class was because they put in one other kid like me in the class. We became fast friends since we were the only one the other could talk to. We were always competing in class, wondering which of the two hands the teacher was going to call on to give the correct answer.

There was only one class that I had with my freshman homeroom class, and that was English. My teacher was Ms. G., and everyday I came into her class late. It was a double period in the beginning of the day. I would usually get there at the end of second period, right before the third period bell would ring for the next class. There were many times when Ms. G. and I would talk about my lateness, and she would seem to sympathize with me. I received a 70 in her class one semester and an 80 the next. I understood the material she was teaching, and if I had attended, I would have been able to catch up with the assignments. But I never did my homework, and I was absent to her class more than I was late. I will never understand why she passed me. I would dodge her in the hallways the days I missed her class because I was too embarrassed to face her.

My schedule was really messed up. I don't think the school knew what grade I was in, because most of my classes were with juniors and seniors. As a freshman, I took Chemistry and was the youngest student. My gym class was filled with crazy horny guys and typical girls trying to get attention from the guys. I had the worst class ever for last period. . . Math B! And, it was also a double period!

Mostly, I didn't really pass my classes while I was in Belmont. Half of the time I was absent, no lie, and the rest, I was late. Every day was a drag and I was getting depressed with the way my school life was going. It's like I lost who I was when I was in school, and it sucked. When June finally came, I knew that it had to be the end. I told most people that I'd never be back, but I didn't really have an idea of where I'd go. I wasn't planning on dropping out, but I didn't really believe that there would be a school that would accept me, especially with my lame grades and spotty attendance record.

When I heard the term "transfer school," I was really surprised. At first I was so glad when I got a high school book that had a handful of schools that accepted students as transfer students. The NYC high-school catalog book was thick, but I was disappointed to find out that of the very few transfer schools, nearly all of them had requirements. You had to be a certain age or an immigrant or something, and it was hard to find a school where I would be accepted.

At the end of the summer, I still had no place to go and there were only a couple schools left to apply to. I couldn't apply until September, when classes would already start. I was so mad, and started school again at Belmont. In my second week of school,

I had an appointment set up with Urban Academy Laboratory High School. One week after the interview, a test, and all the other crap I had to go through to apply, Urban called. Yes! I was accepted, and I would start the following Monday.

expectations
JENNIFER ARZU

By 2005, my sisters were already preparing me for high school. It was no surprise when my mother told me that I would be attending Urban Academy in Manhattan, especially since my older sister Stephanie went here. Her high school experience was one that would be remembered for the rest of her life.

When I first came to Urban to visit with my sister, I didn't even think this was a school. It was so small and had couches everywhere. I soon found out that it was. When I went into the classes, I realized that their way of teaching was very different. The classes were smaller than those at any high schools in the Bronx. When kids spoke, what was coming out of their mouths made plenty of sense. I automatically liked this school. So the following year I applied, and got in with no problem.

second home
NOELLE TANNEN

Urban Academy is the high school I've been attending for the past three years. I entered in tenth grade as a transfer student. Unlike most other places in the country, New York City has specialized schools. Most of these schools circle around a theme, even if the theme is not so great. Urban Academy is a really small alternative school. There are only 130 kids in the entire high school. Unlike most schools, we don't have to take tests, so classes aren't based around taking state exams. Instead, we pick our own classes, which is pretty cool. For instance, I can take something like Russian Literature for English credits. Since our school is so small, it's kind of like a second home. Sometimes I end up staying until six at night with friends. You get to know everyone really well here – people you would never have expected to get to know.

Before I transferred to Urban I attended another high school called Talent Unlimited. It was a performing arts school that taught in the standard "Board of Ed" style, which is more like "Bored" of Ed to me. I wasn't doing so well in Talent Unlimited. I rarely went to school, and when I did it was usually for my lunch breaks or for an occasional English class. My friend Tatiana heard about Urban Academy from the school nurse. She visited the school and told me all about how cool it was. She said there were couches, a ping-pong table, artwork everywhere, a darkroom, and all kinds of things that one would not generally see in a New York City public high school. This really intrigued me so I scheduled a visit. I sat in on some classes and knew immediately that I wanted to transfer as soon as possible. That's exactly what I did.

the last gym class
SOFIJA KULIKAUSKAS

I attended my previous school, Frederick Douglass Academy (FDA), from seventh grade to the first semester of ninth grade. It was a prestigious high school, known for high scores and acceptances to good colleges. On the other hand, if you tell mostly any teenager in Harlem that you go to FDA, they look at you in a different way because of its reputation. FDA is known for a lot of fighting and a lot of drama.

When I went to that school I was the only "white" girl, which caused a bit of a commotion. Some people hated me, and some people were curious about me, and I hadn't even stepped foot in September classes. I didn't understand why a lot of people hated me. Most likely it was because of my skin color. That didn't stop me from going to the school; I saw it as another step in my life with a challenge. I like challenges.

We had to wear a uniform, which was a navy blue skirt or pants, white blouse, and black shoes that were not sneakers. I didn't mind, but if you had something that didn't consist of the right uniform, they would either send you home or to detention for the whole day. That made me upset because you would miss a whole educational day and stay in detention doing nothing, which made no sense since that school was for "excellence." I guess they just went overboard.

I did get caught up in some drama in that school because I had a big mouth and was a bit naïve in certain ways. I didn't learn my lesson until it got to the point where my name was in everyone's mouth, and that school was big. In eighth grade, there were constantly fights, arguments, broken friendships, and heartaches. I witnessed more fights in that school than I ever did before. I was in a few fights as well, and they were definitely not fun. I made a few close friends and many associates or acquaintances.

The beginning of my ninth grade year was hell. I was barely passing, lost in commotion, and constantly getting distracted. I thought to myself, "I can't stay in this school if I want to proceed in life." I wanted to get out of my neighborhood and go to a better school.

My stepfather, Soon Lye, agreed with me. His friend's daughter went to Urban Academy, which was an alternative school. I decided to make big moves and go for it. I applied to Urban Academy in January and went through the whole process of getting interviewed, taking some tests, writing a lot of essays, and – bang, bang, boom – I'm in. When I heard the news, I was in gym class playing hockey. I went to the girls' locker room and called Urban Academy. Cathy, one of the teachers, told me I was accepted. I calmed my nerves, thanked her, and immediately called my mom and told her the great news.

✿

NO uniforms!
FAITH HARRIS

Urban Academy is one out of six schools in the Julia Richman Education Complex. I attended third through eighth grade at the Ella Baker School, another school in the same building. Then I got accepted to a new small high school called Urban Assembly School of Business for Young Women (UASBYW), which opened in the fall of 2005. I wasn't interested in going there, but my guidance counselor at the time suggested it. I figured I should give it a try.

UASBYW was a school that was a challenge to transition into. The dress code was a white button-up shirt, gray slacks or skirt, and the school's personalized blazer or vest. I wasn't used to wearing uniforms because Ella Baker didn't have a specific dress code. The last time I wore a uniform I was in kindergarten. I hate uniforms with a passion because they make everyone look the same. No one can express who he or she really is with uniforms. My mother and I would butt heads all the time because she absolutely loved them. Her argument was and still is that uniforms decrease the competition when it comes to fashion in schools and that they look nice. I totally disagree to this very day.

I really disliked the essence of the school most. Most girls were very catty at times. We only had one floor to ourselves. In a small space like that with a couple hundred girls, things were bound to get heated. In my classes there was a lot of bullying going on, and I didn't like the way the staff was handling situations. Because UASBYW was a new school, it was very unorganized. I needed to get out of that environment and be in a more organized one. When it comes to my education, if I feel a certain way, I'm going to speak up about it.

In the beginning of my sophomore year, I knew I wanted to transfer. In my eyes, I had given the school a try, and I wanted to leave. It was a struggle finding a transfer school. For the Board of Education to remove you from a school quickly there has to be a major issue. For example, if you were in great danger or getting bullied to the breaking point, and you stopped going to school, they would move you out of the area. I was getting frustrated because I really wanted to leave. One option was going to my local zoned high school, Brandeis. I definitely didn't want to go there because of all the myths and urban legends I heard from my mom and her friends who went there back in the day. That's when I went back to my old roots and thought of a plan.

"Urban Academy!" It was perfect, and the school had my name written over all it. It was a transfer school, and I was very familiar with the school. After all it was in the same building I went to the previous six years. Most of all, there were NO uniforms! Thank God! I found the website, called the school, scheduled a tour and an interview, and ever since then my life has changed in every way possible.

YAY! I made it and I'm happier than ever! Urban lets you express yourself in whatever way you want to without fear of getting judged. I've become friends with the majority of people in my school because everyone is amazing in their own different ways. Everyone contributes positive energy to what we like to call our community. I mean everyone might not agree to everything, but that happens in all families. At Urban, many of my dreams came true. Urban was that second chance for me to redeem myself not only as a person but also as a young woman in society. My principal Herb Mack inspires me because he is so dedicated to what he does. He fights for what he believes in. If any principal should get an award, it's him. Good job, Herb!

not some catholic school type
ALYSSA LA CAILLE

Urban Academy is a college-setting high school located on the east side of Manhattan. It was my first time going to school in a different borough. I started at Paul Robeson High School in Brooklyn. I didn't attend that school for more than a week, and noticed I had to leave. I researched high schools, questioned people about where I should transfer to and so on. On my own, I began to search Manhattan. I wanted something different. I was tired of going to school in Brooklyn and hanging with the wrong people, especially in high school. When I saw Urban Academy, read the requirements, and saw how the school setting was, I knew I had to go there. On top of that, it was a transfer school – just what I wished for.

Urban Academy was nothing like what I pictured it to be. I thought it would be on some catholic-school-type vibe, but it wasn't. It was a place where nobody judged anyone, and you were accepted for how you are. I was shy at first, but after a while I got used to it and made friends. Another good thing about Urban Academy was that you were allowed to pick and make up your own schedule. Choosing my schedule felt different to me; I was used to taking my schedule and going to class.

Neighborhood Anthropology was a class I had to take simply because of the neighborhood I live in. I always wanted people to hear about and know how I felt towards my neighborhood, and that class gave me a chance to do so. The class was way harder than I thought, and it took a lot of time. But it's what I wanted so I had to do it.

Urban Academy is a great school, and if you don't think you can take the challenge of being prepared for college then it's not for you. Then again, Urban Academy and the staff can change that. They can prepare you for your future and your goals.

a potential threat
MAKEDA GAILLARD-BENNETT

Towards the end of eighth grade I found out that I would be attending Williamsburg Preparatory High School. I never really attended any schools in my neighborhood. I'm not trying to disrespect the neighborhood schools, but my mother felt that there were better opportunities outside of our neighborhood borders. I was excited by the fact that I'd be entering high school; it would be a whole new start at life, a clean slate. At the end of ninth grade I came to the glum realization that it was the total opposite of what I had expected. Iffy teachers, lousy straight-from-the-textbook homework, and fights seemed to be a part of our daily curriculum. Oh yeah, and metal detectors. Class started at eight-thirty, but they told us to arrive there at eight o'clock to give us enough time to get through the scanners. This was never true. The line was always backed up because some idiot didn't want to give up his or her phone or iPod and slowed the whole line up. The procedure was fairly easy: take off all jewelry, keys, belts, and metal items. They would confiscate anything that was a potential threat. If something happened to tick off the buzzer, a security guard would search you with a hand-held machine. If you still were "a potential threat," you'd have to go behind a curtain. If you didn't oblige they might have to call in a police officer, who was on duty on the premises, and they'd strip search you. I felt like I was in a mini version of prison: trapped and violated.

I knew there needed to be a change in my life – the change that I was hoping and expecting to receive out of a "college preparatory high school." I told my mother my likes and dislikes about the school, and of course the dislikes overshadowed my likes. Yet I wasn't ready to give up my friends that I'd just created.

So ninth grade passed, and eventually 10th, until a breaking point occurred. I *knew* that it was now or never. My creativity and articulate thinking would have gone to waste in a school where a student's opinion didn't matter much. I felt like my school had me trapped. I didn't see any opportunities or advantages. It just seemed like an extension of middle school, but with metal detectors. Eventually, my mother decided that she'd contact the Board of Education and have me placed into a new school. We visited a few schools and noted our disapproval. Before we gave up, my mother told a couple of her close friends – one, a teacher at Urban Academy Laboratory High School – about our search. Hope was in reach. I contacted the school myself and set up a day that I would come in to visit. At the end of that day at Urban, I knew I wanted to be a part of the Urban family.

I found a school where my opinions were valued, and each and every student's personality was welcomed. I was introduced to teachers who actually showed that they cared and didn't give up on their students easily. Yet I still had my guard up. I had my ups and downs adjusting to such a different school. But I knew that this was where I'd get back on the right track. When college time rolls around it will be more than a dream; it will be reality.

❀

"urbanites"
ZAIRA SIMONE

I was attending Legacy High School for Integrated Studies. I laugh whenever I hear its name, because there was nothing integrated about the school's curriculum. Its distinction was that it was located within an office building, overpopulated with 300 students. I recall those mornings of having to wait in line to get in the building because the security guards insisted on checking everyone's I.D. After I managed to make it through inspection, I was already late for class.

I was becoming very frustrated with the school's curriculum. I wanted much more than a traditional-style high school. I was tired of being limited to certain classes like Biology, Algebra, English, and Global History. One class, "Music Management", was created to teach students about the music business. Sad to say, it was the only subject close to performing arts. I guess the school assumed that the majority of its students were aspiring to be rappers, singers, and music producers. More importantly, at times I didn't feel like I was being treated like an individual but rather as a statistic. I began to consider transferring, though I was afraid that I would fall behind in my studies. But one has to make changes in order to move ahead in life, regardless if you experience a few bumps in the road. This became my mantra and I made my way out of Legacy.

I became involved in the International Youth Leadership program, which helps African-American and Latino students develop the ability to apply a global perspective to community and individual challenges. The director of the program advised me to look into small schools. During this time his cousin was looking to transfer to Urban Academy and so he suggested that I also set up an interview. I remember how excited I was when I discovered I got accepted to Urban Academy.

I believe it was around November 28, 2006, at eight-thirty a.m. when I fell in love with Urban Academy. I was becoming infatuated with the seminar-style classes, the debates, and the teachers who continued their lessons outside of the classroom. I gravitated toward classes like African Colonialism, Consumer Science, and Neighborhood Anthropology. As students, we "Urbanites" were encouraged to judge the perspectives of different sources, rather than to regurgitate everything from a textbook. This makes one feel as if their opinions and ideals are valued. The education that I received at Urban was an education that complimented my own interests and life experiences. I have always had my own voice, which has been influenced by these experiences. All of this has inspired me to share my voice in this book.

»INTO THE NEIGHBORHOODS«

Kingsbridge Heights, The Bronx
JULIANNE REYNOSO

A STEP UP

My name is Julianne Reynoso. I'm 16. I was born in New York Presbyterian Hospital in Washington Heights, New York City. It was 12:10 a.m., August 1, 1991. I was one of the first girls in the family; I was my parents' first child, and my grandparents' first granddaughter.

I grew up living with both my parents in the Bronx on Kingsbridge Road between Sedgwick and Kingsbridge Terrace. Before that, my parents and I lived with my dad's parents, my grandparents. They lived in the South Bronx on Westchester Square and Ward Avenue. We were a very connected family; we liked being around each other. We liked to have fun together. Recent years have bumped up my house to a full house; two adults, three siblings, and three pets: a handsome cat named Lucky, Peetie the turtle, and Jerry the dwarf hamster.

We moved into the neighborhood that I live in now in 1993 when I was two. My mother found our new one-bedroom apartment in the newspaper. The rent was only about $475.

The neighborhood was definitely a step up from Westchester Square. In those times, my neighborhood did not have as much drug activity or violence as there is now. Then we moved to a building that was just around the corner; it was a three-bedroom apartment for $650, in a much better building. We have been there 14 years.

I am now in high school. Soon, I'm going to turn 17, and I love hanging out with my friends. I have a boyfriend, a cat, and average grades in school. I still live in the Bronx and my life is pretty great. I love living in New York City, and I don't plan to leave anytime soon. I hope to eventually work helping animals, probably as a veterinary technician.

ON THE PATIO

Growing up, I was always with Roxana Diaz. Her father was the landlord, and they lived on the first floor of my building. I feel it was destined for Roxana and me to be best friends. We were both two years old and had no other siblings or friends. We did everything together. We played tag, or better, freeze tag with the other kids of the building and eventually with our own brothers and sisters. We would play Red Rover for hours, slide on the slides, and create different and more dangerous versions of the games we used to play. For example, all of us would try to get on the same swing and see how fast we could go without anyone falling off. Sometimes two people would swing while others would run back and forth, dodging the swaying bodies coming towards them.

The way my building is structured is that all of the apartments are the same size with a total of only 10 apartments. There are five floors and no elevators. As neighbors in a pretty small building, we are all close to each other. The kids that are in the same age group play together and grow together.

When you walk in front of my building you would never know that I have a back yard. On the side of the main, and only, entrance is a gate that goes down a few steps, and that eventually leads you to the landlord's apartment and into the backyard patio. The backyard faces all of the fire escapes, and every tenant's door is open all summer long.

There were countless summer days when you could catch me in our backyard, running around, playing on the swings. If there was ever a day that I couldn't be outside, it would be most heart breaking. I would be in my room listening from my bedroom window to the kids having fun without me. Roxana would always, always call my name for me to come down, and I would always hear her. I would run to the kitchen and go out to the fire escape and tell her that my mom wouldn't let me because I had to eat soon or we were going to my grandma's house. She would say to please come down, and I would run back to my mom and say that Roxana asked if I could please go down and that I really wanted to go to the patio. And if that didn't work, Roxana would say to bring my mom out on the fire escape so that she could work her magic. And it always worked! They'd be screaming outside together, my mom saying that it wasn't reasonable for me to go down, and Roxana telling her that it was the best idea ever. As soon as my mom would sigh loudly and say, "OK, Roxana!" I would run to my room, throw on my dirty flip-flops, and magically appear in the patio seconds later, screaming the whole way, "I'm here!"

The other people that Roxana and I would play with were my cousin, Miguel, and Kathleen, who was two years younger than all of us. In the beginning, her parents seemed to think that Kathleen was too delicate to play with us. Miguel was my cousin from my mother's side of the family and he lived on the third floor of the building. He was always so restless, jumping off the swings in mid-air and getting hurt every time. He played so rough that, naturally, Roxana would fight him. Roxana, the palest one of us all with her straight, shiny brown hair always cut into a blunt bob, versus Miguel, scrawny with his brown and equally shiny hair styled into a mushroom. It was odd the way it always happened, but we never intervened because they constantly would have these power struggles, arguing whether or not he or she could use this thing or play with this toy.

When we got a little older and Kathleen finally would come down with us to play, Roxana had gotten a cocker spaniel named Diana. Kathy was deathly afraid of it, so of course, we would all make fun of her. Roxana would throw the dog on her and Kathy would scream so much. It was mean, but it was so funny. We would say, "It's just a puppy Ka-ta-leen! Diana won't do anything to you!"

By that time, Miguel and his family had moved out of the building and we were also getting older. We were almost starting middle school and things were starting to change. We were all going to different schools and hung out with our own classmates. We were still evolving and becoming different people. We now all had younger siblings, and they were getting older; their fun was what we *thought* used to be fun back then. Our schools, our different attitudes about things, and the people around us changed us so that we barely even had things to talk about anymore. Eventually I just stopped going to the patio, stopped rollerblading in front of our building, and just stopped hanging out with Roxana. Middle school was a bigger thing than we thought; some of us were just realizing that we could now call our friends on the phone and that we didn't have to lose our contact with them after the school day had ended.

I rarely ever saw Roxana unless we were both at the same party. She would talk about how we should hang out some more, but I usually passed on the offer. I thought that to play those games from before was childish and boring. I now had new and better ways of having fun.

Other times when we saw each other and talked, we talked about when we were younger. There are definitely a lot of wonderful memories stored up inside my building, on the patio. And even though I will eventually leave some of those things behind as I move on in my life, I will never forget the good times with my good friend, Roxana.

MY BRONX

I actually love my neighborhood very much, and it annoys me when I tell people where I live, and they look at me strangely and say, "Wow, you live in the Bronx!" People always assume that the Bronx is such a bad place. Although I must admit that violence does happen (just as much as any place else in New York City), it doesn't happen as frequently as people suspect. There is a mix of cultures living here, and we all get along or just ignore each other.

I live where Sedgwick Avenue intersects with a huge street called Kingsbridge Road. Kingsbridge Road starts on Broadway and 225th Street where the 1 train is and extends to Fordham Road to the B and D trains. Up and down Kingsbridge there are supermarkets, video game stores, discount stores, and bodegas. Small Spanish restaurants, Caridad and Montezuma, dominate the area, cooking greasy breakfasts that we all happily eat.

The apartment buildings are old, brick, and low rising, usually not exceeding six floors. The only slightly higher buildings in the whole area are the Veterans Hospital and the Armory. The Armory, as it's known, is actually named the 258th Field Artillery, and it is absolutely huge.

The neighborhood is filled with many Hispanics, mostly Dominicans or Puerto Ricans, and the competition is rough as proud cultures hang their flags out their windows or shout out in the streets and even through their car windows. In the summer nights, the blocks are crowded as people party and dance in front of their buildings; the music is either salsa or bachata and always loud.

When I finally finish high school and move away, I know I'll definitely miss this place. There are a lot of important spots around the neighborhood; here are some of them:

John R. Brown Triangle is a park across the street from my building, between Kingsbridge and Sedgwick. It's referred to just as "the Triangle" because it's shaped that way. There are many benches, and in the summer people usually just sit there and hang out under the shade of the trees. Older men play dominoes on the tables too, as the Manhattan-Bronx BxM 3 bus passes by. I don't really hang out in this spot, but I have to pass by it every time I go out.

Fort Four Playground is a park up Sedgwick. It has many names, such as "OLA Park," because the Catholic Church, Our Ladies of Angels, is right next to it along with its elementary school across the street. It's also called "143 Park" because Middle School 143 is right across the street, and many of the kids from the neighborhood go there. A lot of people from Sedgwick Avenue hang out in that park and play basketball. There are a lot of skaters, rollerbladers, and BMXers that go there too. I remember many times when I would come out of school and hang out with my friends around the benches, watching the guys play basketball before we would go home.

Deli and Breakfasts, also known as just "Peter's," is a small store right next to Middle School 143. A most-of-the-time-grumpy Asian man named Peter owns it. All of the students from OLA and 143 go there, and he locks all the doors to the drinks and makes sure that if you want to buy something, one of his employees gets it for you so you don't forget to pay. We would always buy the giant baked cookies or blue slushies after school before heading out across the street.

Fort Independence Park also known as "Pigeon Park" is further up Sedgwick Ave. That park is not as popular as the other one, but it's a good alternative if you'd rather be in a quieter place outside. It's a good place to bring little children because it actually has a bathroom and a lot of baby jungle gym things. It's also a great place for tanning because there is a hill with a clearing where the sun just beams on you. You'd be surprised at how many people lie down on blankets in their bathing suits. I don't really come here a lot; it's too quiet for me. I only come here on weekend mornings after jogging around the reservoir because it is on my way home anyway.

Bronx High School of Science has a big courtyard with lots of benches and trees that make shade so students can hang out. It is also a local hangout spot for skaters and BMXers because it's long and flat, making it a great place to practice. This place is known as Bronx Science. I've only been coming here lately because my boyfriend does BMX, and he comes here a lot. It's relaxing and just a nice place to be because it's empty most of the time.

St. James Park is on Jerome Avenue under the 4 train on Kingsbridge Road. It's a big park with a kiddie playground separated from the basketball and tennis courts. There's also a recreational center where kids can play with pinball machines or the air hockey table. There are a lot of benches in the park where people usually hang out and talk 'til late at night. It's sort of dangerous because people get robbed there a lot.

Bronx Library Center is located on Kingsbridge and Fordham and it just opened up last year. It has state-of-the-art equipment and hundreds of computers. This is a hangout spot for odd people who refer to themselves as Emo, Vampires, or just Gothic. They crowd around the entrance of the library in black clouds, talking and smoking. Before, they would go into the Teen Center of the library and cut up the couches. This got them banned from the library, so right now they can only go inside in small bunches. So they mainly just stand in the front. I used to go there a lot when I was in my old school, Roosevelt, when the library was on my route home, but now I only go once in a while.

Fordham Plaza, also known as just "The Plaza," is across the street from the District 10 office and right near Roosevelt High School and Fordham University. There are a lot of small seating areas that look like giant steel balls on the ground with flat tops so you can sit on them. When people cut school, they come here and eat from the vendors that are on the Plaza and talk all day until they have to go home.

Edgar Allen Poe Park is on Kingsbridge Road and the Grand Concourse. Poe Park has Edgar Allen Poe's actual house on its grounds. The park is not that big. Poe's house (or shack – it's so little!) is on one end, a large circular clearing with benches scattered everywhere is on the other end, and a little kid playground is in between. I used to come here often since it's across the street from the library.

High Schools around the area include:
    DeWitt Clinton High School
    Theodore Roosevelt High School
    Kennedy High School
    Marie Curie High School
    Bronx High School of Science

Walton High School
Grace Dodge High School
High School of American Studies

Colleges:
Fordham University
Monroe College
Lehman College

Transportation:
Bx1 bus - Riverdale Avenue to Lincoln Avenue
Bx2 bus - Fort Independence Avenue to Lincoln Avenue
Bx3 bus - Broadway 238 Street to George Washington Bridge
Bx9 bus - Broadway 262 Street to West Farms Square
Bx12 bus - Broadway 207 Street to Co-op City, Bay Plaza
Bx22 bus - Castle Hill to Paul Avenue 205 Street
Bx32 bus - Sedgwick Avenue VA Hospital to Lincoln Avenue
1 local train – Van Courtland Park 248 Street to South Ferry
4 express train - Woodlawn to Crown Heights Utica
B express train - Bedford Park Boulevard to Brighton Beach
D express train - 205 Norwood to West 8 Street NY Aquarium

THE RIGHT SIDE OF THE STREET

My walk home from the subway starts with me getting off the newly renovated Kingsbridge Road train station on the number-4-train line. The side of the street I walk on depends on whether I'm alone or not. If I'm alone I walk on the "safe" side, and if I'm with my friends or boyfriend I walk where the stores are. I do that because if I walk on the side of the stores, the left side of Kingsbridge, I will be looked at and talked to. The right side is where the Armory is at and nobody walks on that side.

If I stay on the right side I usually am talking on the phone or listening to music so I don't have to be aware of the few people around me. The block I walk along is long, and at the end it reaches Reservoir Avenue, a small street that is triangular and has benches along it. There used to be a guy sitting on those benches who was usually staring into the street blankly and mumbling to himself. The kids in my middle school called him Farmer Joe. He was kind of dopey, and the guys in my class used to make fun of the way his shoes "talked"," because the sole had been ripped from the seams, and every time he walked his shoes flapped.

After I walk past his territory, the next block has a chicken spot (a local one, not a KFC), a hardware store, several Chinese businesses, and a lot of grocery stores. There are a lot of people on that block, but they don't hang out there, they're just busy coming in and out of the stores and talking loudly to their friends. Then when I reach the end of the block, University Avenue, I cross the giant street to the other side, then cross again to the left side of Kingsbridge. At this point, I reach a bus stop for three different buses. It's always full of people waiting at the corner. I cross this way because I live to the left side anyway, and the only thing on the entire block is the Jewish old people's hospital.

When I cross the street, the next avenue is Sedgwick. The VA hospital takes up the entire block, from Sedgwick to Webb between Kingsbridge to Fordham, which the front of my building faces. When I finally get to cross the street onto Sedgwick, I arrive in front of my building. Usually there are people hanging around, and I have to make my way past them in order to ring my doorbell, if it happens that I forgot my keys that morning.

Now, let's just say I walk on the left side of Kingsbridge Road. I start at the diner and make my way past a barbershop and fruit shops. Crossing to Davidson, the next street, I come to the corner of a store that used to be a toy store that was never really a toy store, but is now called a beauty supply store and still has Hello Kitty stuff in the windows. Then I pass a furniture store where there is always a man holding the door for people going in and out, knowing that they all have money and really thinking people are going to share their hard-earned cash.

The next store is Subway, which is always empty, so my boyfriend and I always eat there. They are really nice to us because we're regulars and they let us bring our bikes inside. In front of Subway there are always men who I think are Jamaican, sitting and burning incense. Their incense smells so disgusting to me that I always try to avoid talking and even breathing until we've reached the corner of Golden Krust where we know we've safely passed them.

Crossing the street, you'll see a store that sells Pepe shirts and Baby

Phat jeans, and after that is a barbershop with young, cute guys working there. When they're on their breaks they come outside to stand next to the fire hydrant or next to a parked motorcycle that one of them owns. The end of the block is always filled with every kind of old person you can imagine, playing dominoes. They sit on plastic crates all day. The sidewalk makes a large curve, so there is a lot of room for them. On the next corner is a popular pizzeria that is always filled with people because of their delicious pizza and $5.50 mini pies. There are always, always, young guys hanging out in front, eating their slices standing up and checking out the girls passing by. They're either murmuring among themselves or whistling as they break their necks watching the girls from the back.

Another reason that I don't like to walk on this block is because there's a club called La Augila, which means eagle in Spanish. There are always people hanging out there after dark. The club is next to the supermarket Fine Fare, where the street finally curves in to University Avenue, and the rest of my way home from the train is the same.

INTERVIEW WITH JOSE DESCHAMPS

Jose is my boyfriend. He lives in Fordham, which is a neighborhood near mine that actually morphs into Kingsbridge and also intersects with Sedgwick.

Fordham

Okay, Jose. Where were you born?
I was born in the Bronx, on 184th Street by Fordham and Grand Concourse and my

personality is like that place. Life around there is more harsh than any other place, you know, and some place that a lot of people don't want to be or don't really know about. It's very hard over there, and you have to be very strong to survive. You have to be willing do anything to be there, and to get out. That's my main goal – determination all around.

Where do you live?
2395 Tiebout Avenue and before that, I moved from Grand Concourse.

So, generally, you have lived in the Fordham area your whole life?
Yes.

So who did you grow up with? Do you have any brothers or sisters?
I have two brothers and two sisters. I learned a lot from each one of them. And my mom and my dad were there.

school was a puzzle

What kinds of schools did you go to?
Well, the first school I went to from kindergarten all the way up to the fifth grade was Public School 33, and that was a good school. When you are little it's good. After I passed fifth grade, I went to P.S. 115. That's my junior high school. That's where I made a lot of my friends. School was very hard at times. I had a lot of confrontations and had a lot of problems. And I got left back one year because of fighting and being immature. From there, I ended up going to Roosevelt, which was a very bad school at that time. And I had to get out of that school because I was into a lot of issues because many things happened over the summer. So I went to a school called Taft, which was just a little less bad. I was there for a while, maybe until 11th grade. I was trying to keep away from everybody. By that time, there was already a lot of gang-related stuff. The school said you can't wear certain colors. You can't wear red, you can't wear blue – you know, Crips and Bloods – and you can't wear grey. I just wore all the clothes I wanted to wear, and my choice of color was grey all the time. I had a lot of grey clothes. People used to think I was part of

a gang and wanted to pick fights with me and stuff things in my locker. I had to leave that school because either I was gonna stay there and try to graduate as soon as possible or die because I had many confrontations. People put guns to me and threatened my life many times. I don't think it was worth it. I mean, school is very important to me, but my life was more important. So I ended up not going to school anymore. That's what happened.

What sort of confrontations did you get into? Could you be specific?

Many times, people are out to show up. If you have this color on, to them it's like that's their reputation of their gang. If you have the colors and you're not a part of them, it's like you're pretending to be them, and they choose to bother you. You have to be quiet and go down the hall, but they keep on. They want to fight with you, and many times fights start over nothing – for example, just going to gym and changing to gym shorts. The guy next to me was from a gang. He sees me every day in the hallway, and one day he's like, "I don't like you." So I'm like, "You don't have to like me. I'm not your friend, you know." I was going to gym and he pushed me. I'm like, "Hey, you okay? What you push me for?" He kept on, so I ended up hitting him, and from there it's on because, you know, people can't accept defeat. I hit him, and I beat him up, and all his buddies are in that school. At that time I was by myself in the school. I knew nobody; I was new. And they wanted to jump me so I had to cut class to get home early. I didn't want them to hit me or to jump me. It was just many things that were life threatening, you know, and especially since I had no friends there. It was just me, all by myself against everybody, and my family didn't know. I wasn't sharing that with them.

What was the most embarrassing thing that has happened to you?

One summer my friends and I went to a pool. I think it was in Manhattan. It was very hot. Usually we go to Roberto Clemente State Park, but that time we didn't go there because it was already late and crowded. We were gonna meet some girls, you know how young guys do. It was like five of us who have been friends forever; they all lived in my building. I had a brand new pair of sneakers and was all dressed all fly, with my towel and my trunks under my sweatpants. We were swimming for mad hours. We had all shoved all our clothes in a locker because we only had one lock. When we came out to go home, we went to the locker to get our stuff. We found someone had broken into our locker and had taken all our clothes! So we had to go home barefooted with just our trunks and a towel. We had no metro cards or anything to get back home, so we had to beg the policemen. We were all crying; it was mad hilarious. I could never forget that day ever 'cause I was crying like a little bitch 'cause they took my brand-new sneakers, and that was my first day wearing them. They were brand new, out the box, and it hurt me so much 'cause I really loved those sneakers. I saved up months just to buy them. And they took it away from me! I was always hoping I would see the person wearing my sneakers, and if I found out they were a size ten, I would kill him! Just joking.

Who were your best friends? Who were the people that you hung out with?
In junior high I met my friends Mike, Lamar, and Julio. A lot of them are doing good – better than me, but we became friends at that time in that school. I didn't like people getting picked on, and they basically got picked on because Mike is Asian and Lamar is Black. A lot of people like to pick on Asian kids 'cause they book-smart. So they think he's a geek, so I used to defend him all the time. Then we became friends. We all chose to go to the same high school together. We all picked the same three choices, which was Kennedy, Clinton, and Bronx School of Science. None of us got accepted to any of them, so, that's funny, but Mike ended up going to Grace Dodge, and Lamar ended up going to Roosevelt with me. He was in a different class and had a way different schedule from me, so we couldn't see each other that much. So when I was at that school I was by myself, and really, I had nobody there. I'd see them after school. They doing good, going to college. I was just left behind because I had a lot of problems.

Are you still friends with them now?
Yeah, we see each other when we can. I been busy a lot, spending all my time with a lovely girl named Julianne and changing my life, but, I mean, we're very close. They all doing things, working, and I'm working. Mike, I think he say he going back to college, so I

want to go back to school and do many other things, but. . .

That's great. Did you have any bad influences from your friends?

Yeah, I had alot of bad influences. My brother was very popular around my neighborhood because his friends are all big-time drug dealers. And everybody thought that I'm like that, so a lot of people feared me. In junior high I had a big reputation, just rumors, of me being a drug dealer. I never was, but in sixth grade, they made some corny gang called CF, right, and their color was grey, before Bloods and all that stuff came out. So in that school, those kids were bad influences because everybody in the classroom was part of CF, and they used to start fights with random kids. We used to just watch them. I learned from my brother that if people pick on you, you gotta handle that, and then you won't get problems anymore. People think just because you walk in the hallway, they can step on you, push you, and do everything. That's tiring, so sometimes I had fights like that, and sometimes it wasn't worth it. I've learned now that it was a stupid choice, but at that time, it was the only choice I knew. Even now, when I'm riding the bus to work, I see kids acting how we all used to act when we were little because they watching hip-hop stars, and that's how they want to be. But that's not really how those famous people are. You know, they see that gang life. Right now it's died out from how it was in the '90s. It's something that people don't understand, how it really is. They're pretending.

Did you ever get in trouble besides the fights? Did you ever speak back to teachers? Did you refuse to do homework?

For me school was a puzzle. Everything has a wrong and a right way to do it, and it's very simple. Life is not simple always, but, if you could see it correctly, it's very easy. I never got in trouble with teachers that much because, since we had a big, tight group of friends, we used to do homework for each other. We were all in the same classes, but we were good in different things. I was good in math, Mike was good in literature, and we had a Spanish friend who was good in Spanish class. When we all got home, each person would do one of the homeworks, and when we get to homeroom in the morning we all passed the homework to each other and copied it. We'd change like one line or put one wrong answer so it wouldn't look the same. So we didn't have trouble with homework because we was just cheating, you know.

Another time I got in trouble was in computer class; I think it was seventh grade. The teacher was a very mean lady, you know, and it used to be mad freezing: they got a lot of ACs to take care of the computers. In the winter we freeze up in there with the AC on. She wouldn't let us keep our coats. We had to read to ourselves, and so she's reading out loud and then when she calls people's names, like, "Jim, read this," you gotta read that line. Sometimes she used to call my name, and I'm like, "I'm not reading it." I never liked to read out loud. I remember she called my mom, and my brother ended up picking me up. He was so mad, I was scared of him. That was the only trouble I had in school about not doing homework or stuff like that.

How would you like to be remembered?

I'd like to be remembered as someone who finally became a good person. Sometimes I think about heaven. I feel like I've done so many bad things that God would never forgive me. I feel like I'm stuck here. Sometimes I just don't want to be here anymore. It's hard enough. I have to go to work, working harder than anybody else. Everybody else does way better than me because they got a chance to go to college. I'm trying to stop pitying myself and to make more moves and more hustles, you know, to get out of here. To get out of being in the ghetto is very hard. Some people think that they have dreams, and it is something that some kind of dream is there. Sometimes you've been dreaming so hard, but it never comes true, and you give up hope.

So you say you live in the ghetto. Could you describe more about where you live?

Well, my block is constantly something out of a movie, you know. It's something like New Jack City. Many times, even when we were little, we'd go outside and hear gunshots. It's not healthy at all. I have seen a lot of people die. Even now, all my childhood friends from my neighborhood are mostly either dead or locked up. I'm the only one out of all of them that's not locked up or dead. So it's something that's not really easy to understand.

It's something that I never want anybody to go through. It's not good. I never want to share that feeling with anybody because you don't want anybody to go through it. My neighborhood is just drug dealers. Now it's less than before, but it was very heavy back in those times. Sometimes you could be playing basketball or baseball in the courtyard, and some guy who just took PCP or angel dust would act crazy, wanting to just hit people. We'd have to run away from that person before we died, you know. Everybody in the neighborhood was just beating on him because he's going crazy, wanting to kill people and being very dangerous.

Could you speak more about your childhood friends from the neighborhood?
Yeah. There was T---, B---, R---, L---, and C---.They all went to good schools, private schools. They fucked up their lives. They got accepted because of their families. T---'s family was very big on drugs, so they had a lot of connections. I haven't seen C---' in many years, but I heard that he was dating some girl who was sleeping with another guy, so he ended up killing the guy. He shot him a couple of times, and I think he killed the girl too. Now he's in jail for life. And T---, I heard he's in Texas – he's doing good. B--- died recently. He got hit by a car. I heard that R--- killed three guys 'cause they tried to rob him, and he's in jail. I heard L--- is in jail too 'cause he killed somebody. It's crazy. I felt them going in the wrong direction in the beginning, and I didn't want to. I have a totally different lifestyle. I'm not into that.

seeing the light

Why did they go that way and not you? What made you different?
I don't know. Maybe they cannot see a light, I don't know. Maybe some people get into something, and they don't know when to pull out. I saw it was stupid. I was just out having fun, and then I wanted to live better. Sometimes you watch a movie. You see parents and their families so happy, playing board games together and doing a lot of events together. I want it, you know, and I never had it. I wanted to live a very good life, but I had to do bad things to get it. I wanted to live normal, and, I guess, that's what

makes me different.

How have your childhood friends influenced you? What do you think?

I think that without them, I wouldn't end up like now. I would not be here talking to you now. I would be locked up with them. They helped me because hearing this news made me change. I guess I made a good choice, and I'm trying to stay on the right path.

That was great. I'm glad you're here with me now.

I'm glad too.

So who is the most important person in your life?

Besides you, it's me. You always got to love yourself. I guess the most important person is Freddie, my nephew. He's a reflection of me, and that's it.

Why Freddie?

He looks like me. I think he was born to be great. I tried my best to keep him away from everything that's bad. He never had to fight in his life. He never had to do anything in his life. We take care of that for him. He doesn't go to public school; he goes to private. He goes to Cardinal Hayes, and he's doing excellent, you know. He's gonna go to college, maybe be a doctor or a lawyer or whatever. He's working with a Bloomberg firm. He's only 17 and doing great, making a lot of money. He's excellent, and he loves school. He has us and he never had any problems. Nobody ever came and bullied him because they knew what the consequences were. We was there, all of us, me and all my brothers. He looks up to me as a father figure. I just try to give him as much knowledge as possible about the world. I tell him to stay away from the wrong things. I tell him that if he's going to be in a relationship to be very careful to make the right choices.

So what do you say about me?

Well, you very special to me. You changed my life completely because I never thought I could feel this way about anybody. You know it's just – it's something that crazy. It's like an obsession. I quit a lot of things for you, and I try to do my best to make you happy, and I try to be good. Even though we're going through a lot of problems with your family, I'm trying to be strong for us. I'm working my ass off at work, making a lot of money to get us a place so we can start our lives together when you finish school. I'm trying to get everything right.

Tekken and BMX

What is one of the happiest moments of your life?
When I first picked up a joystick. People don't understand what that means. When I was 14 years old, I became very heavily into the gaming scene. I was trying to find who I was. I didn't know yet. I didn't know what I wanted to be. People go to college to figure out what they want to be. That's what they go to college for, right? I was going to school, thinking about being a scientist or mathematics teacher. Through gaming, I met people who just stayed home and played regular games to have fun. I was more into competitive gaming.

When PlayStation first came out, Tekken was one of the first games. It was a fighting game, and I couldn't even afford it. I played in an arcade with a quarter. That's when I first picked up a joystick, and I remember that it was something that was magnificent. I practiced a lot, and I ended up winning tournaments. I won first place everywhere. Tekken 2 came out, Tekken 3, Tekken 4, Tekken 5, and now Tekken 6 came out this year. I quit two years ago.

I was, you know, the number one Jin player in New York City. Jin is one of the characters. I was very heavily into that character. He represents me, who I was. When I dropped out of school, it felt like the right choice because then I had time to be more heavily in the gaming scene, and that's where I was making all my money. There were $500 prizes. That's how I was getting paid. I still love tournaments. Now the gaming scene is so big, they got sponsorships and $10,000 prizes. They have even 100 grand first-place winnings. I'm not doing it anymore. Choices. I want to go back into it, but I'm working now so I don't have time to devote to it. That's the only thing that in my life I felt that I was good at.

Do you have any other hobbies?

Yes, I ride bikes, which some people don't understand. We do tricks with the BMX bikes. It's a whole lifestyle, especially in New York, compared to any other state or country. Over here, we ride brakeless. Sometimes we ride pegless, but mostly we have four pegs and ride brakeless. People don't understand why we got no brakes, but that's the style we have here. We have no brakes because there was one rider sponsored by Animal, a very awesome rider. He lives in Brooklyn and rides Brooklyn banks all the time. He inspired me to go brakeless because it made the bike look so much smoother when he did his tricks. It helped me learn new tricks 'cause you can punk out of the tricks and stabilize the bike faster.

Why didn't he have brakes?

'Cause he couldn't afford it. In his interview he said that he ride with no brakes because at that time he didn't have money. Brakes pop; they mess up. Brakes cost a lot of money to maintain over the whole year. You have to oil them, buy new pads, and constantly clean your rim. It's too much of a headache to make 'em work perfect all the time, and he couldn't afford it. He ended up taking them off, and he rode without it. Then people found other ways to stop other than putting your feet down and riding.

Do you still ride bikes now? Do you have anything else besides riding bikes?

Yes, I still ride now when I get the chance with all my friends, even Mike. We all ride together, and my girl rides too. I play Yugio. It's a card game for kids, but it's pretty good. If I have a son or daughter, I'd like to play with them.

It's good 'cause it's a mathematic kind of game. You be seeing old people, 60-year-old people, playing it. It's crazy. I still got my cards and my decks. That game scene is good too, but I can't continue because I'm working during the tournaments. Everyone has to keep the kids away from the TV all day. They just play with cards on the table, and it's beautiful to watch if you understand it.

Sounds great.

THE GUY WITH THE GREEN BIKE

The first time I ever remember seeing Jose was in the fall of 2006. I was hanging out in OLA Park, and he was riding his bike. I remember specifically noticing him because he looked older, and I didn't recognize him from the neighborhood. He was hanging out with this Asian guy and they were both doing tricks on their bikes.

In October, I was still in Rose (Roosevelt High School). I was dating this guy from the neighborhood. I would wait for him after school because he was on the football team at Clinton High School, and they had practice everyday until 7. Sometimes he would come out early, and I would see him, but most times I would just hang around the park with some friends 'til it was time for me to go home. After a while I noticed that these newcomers on the bikes were regulars, and I would always notice that Jose, the guy with the green bike, was looking at me.

One day I was in the park with my little brother when a girl that I met through a friend talked to me and said, "He likes you, the one in the green bike." She was pointing to Jose while he was riding. I remember clearly saying, "I think he's mad hot too." She obviously told him because he came to me a little while later. He introduced himself as Jose and told me his age, and I'm like damn, he's 21! Mad old! So I lie and say I was 17 even though I had just turned 15 that summer. But a little later into our conversation I told him my real age, and he said it was cool. He said that he had always thought I was young, but since he saw my little brother, he assumed it was my son and that I was older. We talked for the rest of the day until it was time for me to go home.

From that day on I would see him more regularly. By then I was already in Urban and was in my first photography class. I chose to take pictures of the BMX scene, and Jose and his friends were my main subjects. I would take some pictures of the other riders he was friends with. I never really paid much attention to his friends because they didn't like me. I knew this because none of them even showed the slightest interest in me, even though we were already dating. I eventually found out that they didn't like that I was taking up all of Jose's time and that he barely hung out with his friends because he was with me. I didn't care, because I don't like anyone who doesn't like me.

Millbrook Projects, The Bronx
JENNIFER ARZU

ABOUT ME!!!

Jennifer, I hate that name

It brings my personality to shame

But like others before me it seems to be the name doesn't make the

Person.

My 'hood mentality and

Wits

Came from the streets and for that I am thankful.

Millbrook taught me that putting my trust in people can, and will, be your downfall.

It taught me that guys will tell you anything to get what they want no matter

Who gets hurt in the process.

That's why I'm glad to have my friends, cousins, and family.

I love my home.

I didn't really start noticing my sisters and brother until

I went to 7th grade.

Weird huh?

As I grow I

Take

Each of their styles and personalities and

Make it my own. I'm

Patient,

Understanding,

Hot-headed,

Smart,

Beautiful,

Brave,

Curious,

Funny and

Gangsta –

LOL!

People in my life and neighborhood shaped and molded the person you see today. . .

GREETED BY A DOZEN

When you first come into my apartment you're greeted by my puppy, Molly. Even if she doesn't know you, she jumps up, ready to attack. She leaps up until you give in and pick her up, and if you do, get ready for a whole lot of licks and tender lovin'. Molly's the cutest thing in the world. She looks like a wolf and hops around like a rabbit. When you're done being formally welcomed at the door, the smell of my parent's food drags you in like a bee to honey. When I say my parents, I mean either my ma or pa because my mom normally cooks, but sometimes when my father comes from his job, he gives the kitchen a test drive (giving my mom a break). Now what you have to understand is that my ma and pa make different types of foods. My ma makes the usual arros con pollo y abichuela (rice with beans, chicken, and other fabulous taste-filled meals) while my papi cooks jerk chicken, pernir, and other concoctions which I do not know the name of. My dad brings more variety to the table (well, not really the table because we all eat on the couch). My mom makes the same things, but her food always comes out wonderfully delicious. We can all tell the difference between their cooking, so we make sure not to thank the wrong person.

There is a second exit to the kitchen with a square glass table right in front. Its tempting fruits, such as bright yellow bananas, full-size mangos, and red shimmering apples, are gently placed in a crystal bowl, which shines whenever we decide to let the sun come in. There are exactly five wooden chairs positioned around the table. Next to it there's a wooden cabinet that holds gorgeous treasures including my mom's priceless white and silver dishes, crystal champagne glasses, and captivating teacups.

Beyond, there's the living room with burgundy sofas that match the rest of the furniture. A small coffee table in the center of everything contains a green glass vase and fake roses.

A while ago, the other blue glass vase broke because my older sister went on a rampage. She was upset that my younger sister had been "disrespectful" to my mom. They don't fight like that anymore, but crazy things tend to happen in that living room. If it's not a flying shoe, Molly is doing back flips. There are discussions that will never leave the apartment, talking back to the elders, belt whippings, rolling eyes, finger snapping, and egg fights.

Whenever I get upset with my older sisters I tend to roll my eyes and suck my teeth, which I know they hate. When my older sister talks about how I "should always listen to my parents," it normally goes in one ear and out the other. As she continues to talk and talk and talk, I try really hard not be disrespectful, but a lot of the times it comes out without me wanting it to. That gets me into even more trouble, causing me to sit through another lecture. . .

Two times a week my dad never fails to tell us about the importance of a good education. He tells us that my mother and he came to this country for us. They won't always be around to take care of us so we have to prepare for the future and live our lives well. That means no boys until we move out, finish school (all of it, including college) and get a "good" job.

In the hallway you see pictures of my grandmother (my mother's mother). In my favorite, she is gazing up at the sky with her smooth, baby-soft skin, ruffled striped shirt and French-braided gray (almost white) hair. To your left, there's the bathroom with its abundance of clothes overflowing from the hamper and the fogged-up mirror. There's always someone taking a shower.

To your right there's my brother's room, which surprisingly is always clean. He cleans up after himself, and, other than the shoes on the floor, everything is in its place. Also on your right there's my bedroom. Unfortunately I share it with my younger sister, who is a hot mess. Beware of all of the untidiness. Sometimes when she leaves her clothes on the floor, I just throw them out into the hallway. Our beds are across from each other, so the room is kind of split in half. My side has all my artwork, paintings of weird faces and different worlds, and magazine cutout collages. My shoeboxes are all located in the corner by my full-

length mirror (which I have to look at every morning at least five times before heading out).

Then there's my parents' bedroom. All I can say is that it seems like it gets bigger everyday.

When you depart, you are pursued down the hall by Molly, who pounces up and leaps up until you give in and pick her up, and if you do, get ready for. . .

INTERVIEW WITH JESSICA, MY SISTER

The Bronx

My name is Jessica Arzu, I am fourteen years old and today is May 3, 2007. Location is Grand Central Terminal in the StoryCorps Booth, and I'm here with my sister Jennifer, so today she is going to be getting at me.

Where did you grow up, Jessie?
I grew up in the South Bronx. Middlebrook Houses, like, the regular 'hood. I lived in the projects. I like it. I like the people and the way it's set up. I like the parks on the side. You have the store. Everybody knows everybody. Everybody gets along. Well, not everybody because I don't get along with a lot of the girls there. I usually get along with the guys.

How do the people act there?
Can I say ghetto?

Yeah, you can say ghetto.

Yeah. Basically like that.

You like hanging around ghetto people?

I don't mind. I don't really care how you act; I get along with a lot of people.

How's your relationship with your parents?

My mommy likes my youngest brother more than she likes me. It's okay because she pays less attention to me, so I can go a lot of places without her noticing. The same goes with my other sisters. I noticed when my sisters were growing up, my mother paid a lot of attention to me because I was the youngest.

What are your siblings like? If you could describe all of us in one word, especially me, what would it me?

My oldest sister Gina is really generous and smart. She's there when I need her advice. I like her a lot, but she needs to move out. My second oldest sister, Erica, is really funny and also intelligent. I like her too. And Stephanie, my third oldest sister is really independent. Jennifer, she's sassy and fragile and really sensitive. I have to say certain things around her that I won't say around her friends because she's just really sensitive. My youngest brother is a brat. He's really spoiled. We get into fights most of the time but he's okay.

Do you get into a lot of trouble around your neighborhood?

No. To get into a lot of trouble, you have to mess with a lot of girls there, and I don't talk to a lot of girls because of the way they act. I don't associate with a lot of females there.

How do you picture your neighborhood in fifteen years?

I think it's going to be the same because I see the little boys there now and they act like the older boys. They take them as role models, and I'm just thinking they're going to be the same way in a couple of years.

What are you most proud of?

I made it very far without falling behind in grades and stuff.

I only got held back once and I'm really proud of that. I just want to keep up the good work. I don't want to slack off.

Did you ever disobey your mother?
Well, not all the time, but most of the time. I do a lot of things behind her back. She doesn't know though, because she doesn't pay much attention to me since she's the only parent at home.

Then again, you have your oldest sisters that watch over you. They treat me like they are my mother. Some of the time it's good, but most of the time it's like, back off, you stupid bitch.

Just last Saturday when we went to go sneak out. Yo, that was like a freaking movie. We wanted to go and sneak out the house.

We had five minutes to go to the store and we went to the party. We made it back on time and nobody said anything.

The only thing was, we smelled like smoke. We weren't smoking but we were hanging out with people that smoke. And we was just chillin' there, dancing, whatever.

Yeah that was so funny. We only had a certain amount of time and we had to make it back. Nobody noticed anything because, like, a family was there. Then we came back home, and we left to go to another party. But yeah, how would you describe yourself now?

I have more respect for myself. I don't care a lot about what people say. If you don't like me for who I am, then fuck you. Now I'm really independent. When I was younger I used to latch on to other people and say, "gimme this, buy me that, can you come with me to this place because I'm shy?"

Do you love or hate your neighborhood?
I love my neighborhood because I get a lot of attention. The females don't like me but I

don't really care. I don't start any trouble. It's probably because my older cousin is really, really, really popular. My mom is planning to move but I really don't want to move. I want to stay with my cousins.

I would want to move. That neighborhood is not doing anything for me. I want to go to somewhere better. I don't like the projects.

It's not about that. It's about having a home.

I like my home. Everybody knows everybody. Everybody knows everybody's business.

It's really diverse. I like that because I met a lot of people from different countries and different backgrounds. I didn't even know people that were mixed with this and that. It was crazy.

[StoryCorps Interviewer] How would you explain your neighborhood to somebody who's never lived there?

It's really homey. People talk to you out of nowhere. You get to know different people that you didn't know. You thought stuff about them. You thought they were this and that.

Yeah. And you get to know them and it's like. . . wow!

Yeah, like, "my perspective of you is really different now."

You think people there are kind of dumb sometimes but –

But they're really smart. People in my neighborhood have talent.

Yeah. They just don't put it to good use.

Yeah they don't. It's kind of congested too. You hang out with the people. You come home, and you chill at the basketball courts, because that's where everybody is at. You just talk to your friends, walk your pit bull or something.

It's kind of like a big family kind of thing. Word.

[StoryCorps Interviewer] Why do you want to leave Jennifer?

I just want something different. I don't want to be there anymore. I've been there for sixteen years. I just want to move, see other things and experience how it is to live somewhere else. I want to do it now. I want to live in a house.

[StoryCorps Interviewer] Was there ever a time when you guys were like, "I don't like the projects?"

Sometimes. If you do something you will have a reputation. That's the bad thing because everybody will find out. Next day, everybody would be like, "Look at her." That happens in school too. You can't really avoid that.

[StoryCorps Interviewer] What did you guys used to do when you were younger? Do you remember the games you used to play?

Hide and Seek in the dark.

Yes! All the time. That was so much fun. We just invented that game out of nowhere, didn't we? It was dark and we were just like, "'Let's play Hide and Seek in the dark." Now my little cousins and my little brother play it, but we don't want to now because we're older. We would make tents and stuff with the bed sheets and the bunk beds. We would make little houses and play house. We would pretend that there's lava on the floor, and we would have to jump from the bunk bed to the other bed. "Don't step on the lava or you'll die."

We still hang out all the time; it's just that now we don't play games. Now it's parties and hanging out with friends, older people. That's cool.

Going out shopping. I'm taking a knitting class now. I'm fascinated, it's really cool. I like making things like purses, hats. I made an arm warmer one time and I still use it. In school they provided some materials for us, so I made it a hobby. I go out and buy yarn and needles to do my own thing now.

I like to play basketball but I don't know how to play right.

She likes to sing in school on the piano. Like, I'll play the piano and she'll sit on top of it. She'll just sing and she thinks she knows how to sing but –

I do! I do!

Shhh. And during lunch, all of our friends would laugh because she thinks she's this diva that she's really not.

Sometimes I really want to go out of state, like, I wanted to go to Atlanta for college. But I don't know how much it would be. I think it would be more money.

And don't forget about family because our family is so close. You see our cousins every now and then. Most of the time we're with them when we do things like barbecue and party.

I don't want to miss out on that either. But it's your education, so sometimes you have to choose. I don't know, but do you think it would be different if we went to a high school in the Bronx?

Yes, more problems with females. I've been to schools in the Bronx for elementary, and they love to start fights for no reason.

family

[StoryCorps Interviewer] Who is the most important person in your life?

My parents. They support us a lot. Especially my mom.

Yeah. And my dad, yeah.

Especially for a single parent, she does a lot. I notice. That's why I feel like I have certain responsibilities around the house to help her because she goes through a lot. My father, he comes home every five months, because he works as a merchant seaman. Every six months, but he does a lot for us too.

And I know he's away just to support us so –

You can't be too mad.

Yeah, basically. And when he comes home you can't bother him because he's tired.

He needs his rest but he does a lot when he does come home. He cooks, and his food is really good, and when we need to ask him for money, he's there. Also my mom. She put two of my sisters, like, one is in college right now. She pays a lot of money and stuff.

But yeah, they're really important to us. All of my parents.

Yeah.

[StoryCorps Interviewer] If you could say anything to them now, what would you say to them?

I love you.

[StoryCorps Interviewer] Can you tell me the happiest time in your life and the saddest time in your life?

Probably when I went to Honduras.

Everywhere you go there's family.

And its like, "that's your cousin over there," like, wow! I love the house over there and stuff.

The house and the backyard. Everything we can't have over here we have over there. And we go on vacation right after school is over.

Yeah, it's a good life. I like it. I have no worries. The only thing is – my only job is to go to school –

Go to school, accomplish what we need to do and stuff. I just want to go to college and get a real good job.

Sometimes I feel like getting life over with. I just want to skip high school and go straight to college.

People do change, like, look at Ma. She used to go out to clubs in high heels, short dresses, and my father went to parties. Now she's like a devoted Christian. She goes to church, like, four times a week, and mainly she can't miss a Sunday because she'll regret it and feel really bad about it.

She's just sweeter I guess. She pulls our family together.

And my older sister too. She's a devoted Christian too. She actually got my mom into Christianity. We go to church from time to time.

On Sundays? I go visit my friends but, you know. I go visit my friends and do my homework. I do my homework on Sunday but at night, around 10. I just leave it for the last, last minute. Even if I'm not doing anything on Saturday I still wait 'til Sunday. How do you think the schools in our neighborhoods are? Do you think the teachers care?

You don't see them talking to students after school. Like, "You're doing this wrong," or

"You need to get your stuff together." At Urban Academy, you don't even have to ask. They'll come up to you and tell you, "You're not doing this; this is what's going to happen to you." Like, get your stuff together. They're always behind your back. And we have mailboxes and they'll leave letters in there. And on Tuesdays and Wednesdays we have tutorial. And teachers actually sit down and talk to you. Like, "What are you doing, what work do you have? If you have work, do it right now I'll help you."

They actually sit down with you and help.

And in all the classes, the maximum number of students is fifteen. So you get individual attention. So I think that's really great.

[StoryCorps Interviewer] If you can say something to yourself in the future, because you'll probably listen to this when you get older, what would you say to yourself 10 years from now?

I just don't want to do anything that I'll regret.

Just basically: stay on my stuff and be responsible, because that's one thing right now I'm not good at. Responsibility. I'll tell myself to be responsible –

And when you graduate, give Mommy and Papi half your check.

And stick to family.

Don't forget your family. They're really important.

A TASTE OF MILLBROOK

When first waking up on a bright Saturday morning I already wonder, "How will my day go – dreary, exciting, or dull?" Whatever the case, I know one thing. The noise and the joy of kids playing Double Dutch and the sweaty teenage boys bouncing their basketballs let me know that everything is going to be all good. I awake, perform my daily wakeup ritual and slip into my navy blue Capri's, white tee, and baby blue pearls. I walk towards my living room to greet my family. The only reason I am not outside yet is because nothing is going down at this time. It's only two o'clock (yes I do wake up at two p.m. sometimes). Everything is poppin' at seven p.m. on the dot exactly, when everybody comes out to have fun with his or her friends and joke around.

When leaving my apartment, I smell the urine on the elevator floor, so I open the door to my front lobby to smell the fresh air. Sometimes it smells like flowers and puppies, but it can smell like dog crap or garbage. The lobby doors are steel with locks, so to get in you need either the key or a code. It doesn't matter because people that don't live there somehow get in. They just built a scaffold because construction workers are repairing the roof. It's there just in case someone or something falls. People in my neighborhood love the scaffold. It gives us shade and we can sit and climb on it.

My friends around the Millbrook projects consist of only males, unless my cousins Johana and Kathy come over from Burke, which is in the Bronx but not in Millbrook. I only recently started hanging with my 'hood friends. My sister, Jessica, formally introduced me. Hanging out with them around my neighborhood can be rough because they don't have such a great reputation. I really like my friends' personalities, humor, and thinking. I remember one dark and humid night; we were all outside waiting for a party to start. My cousins, sister, and friends were just chatting away (mostly about nothing), when suddenly, we all heard gunshots. We were scared and worried for one another. All I remember is us running away from where we had seen flashes of light. We all ran until we reached my block, exhausted.

Even though I happen to love my neighborhood and the various characters in it, not everyone in my family feels the same way. My parents are doing everything possible to move us out of the Millbrook projects. They feel like we don't belong, and that we stayed here longer than we were supposed to. My parents feel we deserve better. They don't like the gunshots that are fired at night. They are worried that their kids might not come home one night or the girls might get too involved with these "hooligans" and get knocked up.

OBSERVING MY ZONE

I have mixed feelings about my neighborhood. Sometimes I don't like it, but at the same time I wouldn't want to live anywhere else. One of the reasons I don't like it is because in the summer the heat is unbearable. I guess that is because all the buildings are so close together the rays from the sun heat the inside of the projects. That's one of my many theories. I don't know if it's true or not.

One of the reasons I like it is because the people around me make it fun. My friends are funny, crazy, and basically say what they want, no matter what. My sister and I chill with them in the big park in back of my building. It's easy making new friends around there because my friends just invite their friends over, and we all have a good time together.

Another reason why I like my neighborhood so much is the big park. It's known as "the basketball park" because it has four full-size basketball courts. Everyone comes from everywhere, but the only other project that's invited is Cypress. The basketball park is split into two by a gate. One side consists of a slide (this section is for the kids), monkey bars, and two dolphins that squirt out water in the summer when it's hot. The other side has many benches (this part is for the teens and the adults who sometimes play basketball) and basketball courts. The basketball park is not only somewhere I go because my friends are there, but it's also a place I can think about private stuff. This happens only at night when it's quiet.

The park has its little moments when people from other blocks come and start problems. This happened on many occasions, but there was one specific moment when there was a shootout and this dude got shot. They say it was because this dude's girl already had a man – NOT just a man, but a husband. The husband shot the boyfriend. It's really pathetic to fight over a woman. Even if it were me, I would still say it's not worth taking a life over.

Boys will be boys. Speaking of boys/men, one of the other reasons I don't like my block is because the boys are disrespectful sometimes. As soon as the weather starts getting good, you see guys in front of their building just waiting for a girl to walk by, whispering and whistling at us like we are dogs. The female could have on a bandana and some baggy sweats and could smell, but the guys would still try to bag that. I swear guys can be hounds. Even the old ones try to talk to you. You could look 16 and be 13; you could look 12. They could be saying "hi" to your mother one day and the next they could try to talk to you in an inappropriate matter. Where I live, anything goes.

The females are another problem. I don't really hang around with the females because they are stank and act like birds. When referring to a female as a bird, it simply means that she is loud, ghetto, and walks around with an attitude. They think they are better than the girl next to them. They are two-faced and too loud for my liking. I really don't know why a lot of them don't like me. I guess it's because they know what I think of them. I must admit I can have my bird moments too, but what girl doesn't? It's just all too. . . complicated. Why does it always have to be a competition with us females? Why do girls have to hate on each other? Why can't we compliment each other or hug one another?

*   *   *

I've been observing my zone further, and with a watchful eye, I have come to understand and love my neighborhood. Before I did not understand the people, the way my community functioned and runs, but now I have a clear understanding of it.

When becoming aware of and observing the men around my neighborhood, I see the guys can be rude and obnoxious, but if someone from another block is insulting or barking at you, they'll be the one's to back you up. They would defend you. There's a sense of communication. At the same time there's like a code that only the guys on your block can try to bag you or something like that.

The females aren't that big of a deal anymore. They're more concerned about impressing the guys than they are about me. There are a few of them that hang in the old crusty basketball park by my building. As soon as there's a game, every girl is down there cheering for her make-believe boyfriend.

THE REAL SURPRISE PARTY

The summers around my way are crazy cool and filled with drama. Summer is the time to find out who's doing whom and to stay out really late without your parents' permission. Summer's the time to catch up with friends you haven't seen all year. Maybe you have seen them, but just said "hi" and "bye" because you were too busy to say anything else.

The summers in Millbrook are like a *Rugrats* adventure (you never know how it is going to turn out until the end of the episode). For instance: On a late July night my cousins (Kathy, Johana, and Emily) came to sleep over. We went outside to stroll around. That's when we happened to stumble upon one of my friends, who was 14 at the time. He had invited us to a party, and told us there would be older people there. We were all 13 and wanted to be at the parties with the older teenagers. Of course my mom said "no" as usual, but we went anyway. My dear mother had to go to church at eight p.m., so we thought sneaking out was no problem for us. Getting past my three older sisters was not an issue at all. So at ten o'clock we waited for all of them to fall asleep. Take into consideration that they were, still are, and GOD willing will always be, deep sleepers. Not even the thunder of Zeus or the sweet sound of Orpheus' voice could wake them up.

So our plan was coming into play WHEN ALL OF SUDDEN THE DOOR FLEW OPEN! In just a matter of seconds, the expression from our faces went from peace, bliss, and satisfaction to that of confused little girls asking mommy to play just one more hour in the park. IT WAS MY MOTHER. She said "CANSELARON LA BIJILIA," which means, "Service was cancelled." Those horrible words pierced through my heart like swords (yes, it was that serious). As we waited for Mother to sleep (which only took about ten minutes) we tried not act too suspicious. We were like pros. Well, we almost were. We had our "real" outfits in our bags and our money stacked.

We were hoping that no one would hear the creaking door as it was flung open by my rough and heavy-handed cousin. She apologized time and time again as we made our way into the outside world of violence, loudness, and extreme chaos. I observed the viejitos (old folks) all up in our faces and boys trying to get our attention by play fighting or almost breaking their necks to see who was coming out of building 165. We kept going to our destination, across the street to building 169. The party was going to go down in just a matter of seconds. The next block was screaming with excitement, guys chasing each other with canes, bicycles running over people, dogs disobeying their masters, and kids scampering into the street without their parents' consent. Other than that, everything was going smoothly.

When we reached 169 we could already hear the music from the fourth floor: "Mamacita" by Collie Buddz and "Freak-A-Leek" by Petey Pablo. Already singing along to the songs and dancing to the music, we approached a fat man with long jet-black hair who smelled like Old Spice, standing in front of the door, charging a dollar. He was clearly Puerto Rican because of the flag that was stretched out across his chest. We bumped, knocked down, and charged through people. A lady ran across the dance floor. In my opinion this was really unnecessary because her huge lard was already downing innocent bystanders for no apparent reason at all. To our surprise this enormous lady turned on the lights. When this incident happened, our eyes widened, we screeched in horror. At that point in my youthful life I felt worse than death. My cousins and I towered over these midgets! At that moment we only cared about our reputations. We sophisticated, attractive, hip young women were surrounded, not by glamorous grown-up teens, but by mere 12 year olds.

We bolted towards the door, which was now glowing like the entrance into heaven. We made it out with no problem. When we made it downstairs we broke out into hysterical laughs realizing that we were really only 13. We were upset because of all of the trouble we had been through to get up to that specific point. It was all worth it, though. Moments like this are what make my neighborhood memorable.

Inwood, Manhattan
NOELLE TANNEN

A FAMILY OF ARTISTS

My name is Noelle Tannen. I am 18 years old and I live in New York City. I was born on February 25, 1990, in Lenox Hill Hospital on the Upper East Side. I feel as though growing up in NYC gives me a sort of edge. I don't mean to sound like an elitist or anything, but this statement stands strong. Whenever I go places and I tell people that I'm from New York, they automatically treat me with this sort of dignified respect. I suppose it's because New Yorkers are so innately aware of their surroundings. Through my life I've been exposed to so many different types of cultures and people. Geographically this city may be small, but it does have one of the largest populations. Growing up in New York makes it impossible to identify myself with one particular culture. I identify myself as a New Yorker, one who is open to all.

I come from a family of artists. My mother is a cellist, and she comes from a line of classical musicians. My father used to be an actor, but now he runs an organization called TIPA, which stands for Toward International Peace Through the Arts, and was just nominated for the Nobel Peace Prize. His father was an entertainer. My sister is a writer. I write music and act. Art is my life. There is nothing in this world that keeps me together more than writing music and performing.

They say it's the events in your life, your experiences, that make up who you are. I suppose there is a lot of truth to that. However, lot of what makes me who I am is the people I have known throughout my life and the relationships that I have built. I haven't sustained all of them, but there is no doubt that they made me who I am today.

The first best friend I ever had was Shelya. I was three when I met her, when I lived in Rego Park. We went to preschool and elementary school together. She would come over to my house. We would spin around on my Sit 'N Spin and play with Barbie. We would hang out with the other

neighborhood girls and pretend to be the Spice Girls. I'll tell you one thing, that girl was a very deep three year old. She would tell me about Korea, the people struggling there and how she felt for them. She told me that everybody in Korea was her family. I thought that was amazing, to have a whole country for a family.

My sister was also a huge part of my childhood, probably because I spent so much time with her. She is nine years older than me, so we were always going through different stages of life. She taught me how to be optimistic. She would pick me up from school almost every day and make me do my homework, no matter how much of a struggle it was. On my birthday she would do it for me. We would watch all the five-o'clock TV shows like *Fresh Prince of Bel-Air* and *Full House*. Her friends would come over and hula-hoop longer than anyone else could.

When I was 14 I met a group of girls: Juli, Ariana, Tatiana, and Marcela. We were so young, but we thought we were so old and mature. It's kind of funny. We were all so different, yet we all had one thing in common. We knew what a good friend was. Whenever something was off with any one of us, we were there to comfort each other. We would be free of all the seriousness in the world. It didn't really seem to matter at all. One of my friends made me realize that you can't just sit around and wait for things to come your way. If you actually get up and do something about what you want, more than you ever thought of will come your way if you are patient. Without these people I wouldn't be as open as I am today. I think that's what life is all about, being open to different ways of living.

"HARRY POTTER" OR "SORCERER'S STONE"

In 1999 my sister Shamie graduated high school. She moved to London for college, and my mother entered the School for Strings grad program in Manhattan. My mom

always said that once Shamie finished high school we would be moving to Manhattan, and that's exactly what we did. My mom always hated living in Queens, as did my sister. Personally I was too young to even care. Rego Park was not really a place to me; it was more of an experience. It was never as dull in my eyes as it was to my sister and mother. Everything is a lot more exciting when you're a kid.

We moved to Rego Park when I was 3 years old in 1993. At first my sister and I attended a Lutheran school down the block from our apartment. One day in kindergarten I came home to report to my mom that Jesus was coming. The next year I attended public school.

In Rego Park we lived across the street from a deli pizza place, a Chinese joint, and a restaurant called London Lenny's. There was a 7-Eleven down the street, and the rest of the neighborhood was pretty much occupied by the cemetery. We lived right above this old couple, Wanda and Sunny. Wanda hated us. In a neighborhood that consisted mostly of all old white retired pharmacists, my mom always said that we stuck out like sore thumbs. We were a family of three females that had three different last names. My mom always had a cello on her back, my sister and I are of two different races, and I made more noise than a marching band. Wanda would call the cops every time I ran around the house and my mother practiced the cello. My mother use to tell Shelya and me that her name was "Wanda the Witch," and she flew around the block with her broomstick at midnight. Being the gullible four year olds that we were, Shelya and I were quick to accept the myth. One time Shelya and I had to go down to Wanda's apartment with my mother because she was complaining about the noise we were making. Shelya walked up to Wanda and asked, "Is it true you're a witch?" Wanda looked shocked and asked Shelya why she would ask her such a question. "Elvira my mother told me so," she said. Wanda was pissed.

So, after six years of living in Rego Park, it was finally time to leave. The only problem with Manhattan was that it was quite possible that in order for us to afford the rent, we would have to live in a bad neighborhood. That's where Inwood comes in. Inwood was a discrete little neighborhood located on the upper tip of Manhattan. It was not a bad neighborhood; however, not many people even knew it existed. We traveled two hours from Rego Park one day and took the A train all the way to the last stop (207 Street). When I got off the train, I didn't think that it was bad, but it was definitely nothing like Rego Park.

There was Spanish music blasting through the streets and lots of stores, compared to where I used to live. When we got to 204th Street, I remember seeing a bodega with lots of guys standing out front, a pizza place, a drug store, a flower shop, and a laundromat (and that was only half of one block). When we finally entered the building, I saw a huge entrance, like a really deep tunnel, with "Hawthorne Gardens" engraved on the top. When I walked through the tunnel, I could hear my voice echo. Once I got through the tunnel, I saw clay lions in front of every entrance within the building. My mother told me to say "Harry Potter" if I liked the apartment and "Sorcerer's Stone" if I didn't. We entered the apartment on the first floor, the landlord showed us around, and I replied with a "Harry Potter."

A month later we moved in. For some reason my mom wouldn't let me be a part of the moving process. She sent me up to New Jersey to stay with my aunt Gulia for the weekend. To this day, I don't know why. When the weekend was over, Gulia drove me to Inwood. I walked into our new apartment to find all the remains of our old apartment scattered around the new environment.

Settling into the new apartment took some getting used to. My mom and I both slept on a big bed in the living room until she moved into the bedroom. Our television didn't work for a while because in Manhattan, you have to pay for cable unlike in Queens back in those days. It's kind of funny; people would think I was crazy because I didn't have a working TV in my apartment.

To tell you the truth, I didn't really care much for Inwood when I first moved in. It actually hasn't been until recently that I've really become aware of it.

LAUNDRY, FRESH AIR, MARIJUANA, & CIGARETTES

When I first moved to the neighborhood, it seemed pretty crazy because it was a lot different from Rego Park. It is a lot rawer. When I say raw I mean real. It is louder and busier. There aren't as many old people, and the few that live in Inwood are usually drunk. It's also a lot more ghetto. I like it, though. When I was younger and first moved here, I wasn't very connected to the neighborhood. It was a comfortable place to live, but I went to school downtown on 92nd Street, so I spent a lot of time there. When I was uptown I spent most of my time inside my apartment. My mom was over protective; she didn't even let me go to the corner store by myself until I was 12.

I remember this man that owned a laundromat next door to my building. He was a veteran from Vietnam, and he had lost his arm there. He has lived in the neighborhood since even before he went to war. I used to think he was homeless, but he's not, just kind of crazy. About four years ago the laundromat was shut down. Some say it's because he was caught with drugs in the back office, maybe marijuana, but I'm not sure if that's true. I didn't see him for years after that. There's this other man that I've always seen in the neighborhood. I don't know his actual name. He's a drunk. He's crusty, but I don't think he's actually homeless. The man carries a radio with him and sings along to the tunes in a drunken manner. I don't think he'll ever leave Inwood.

I also always noticed the loud Dominican music playing through the streets. The Dominican culture is a big, vibrant part of what the neighborhood is and has been since as long as I've been there.

As I've grown older and more independent with my own ideas, I've come to see what the neighborhood is really about. It is extremely chilled out in Inwood. Hardly anybody bothers anybody. I don't really feel like I have to prove myself. I love how accepting it is. There are a lot of different groups of people: yuppies, gangsters, immigrants, old drunk Irish men, drug dealers, and the Dominican community. I'd feel comfortable approaching any of these groups of people and hanging out with them. I know that a lot of people feel this way about the neighborhood as well, from what they say. There are hardly any police around bothering us like in Harlem or anything. We manage to keep ourselves together for the most part.

You can also get the cheapest stuff around Inwood; down by Vermilyea Avenue, the clothes are ridiculously cheap. I bought a pair of really nice skinny jeans for only six dollars.

Over the past 10 years, there has been a lot of gentrification in the neighborhood. More and more trendy restaurants and college students have been moving in. I think it's because of Washington Heights.

"The Heights" have been more and more gentrified and trendy for years already, and since it's just right below Inwood, I'm pretty sure it just spread.

The one thing I can't stand about my neighborhood is the sleazy men on just about every corner, hitting on girls young enough to be their daughters, especially late at night. There have been a lot of sexual harassment scandals in Inwood. So it makes me kind of scared when I'm coming home late at night and there's a group of men almost twice my age basically shouting at me.

One thing that's quite apparent to me about my neighborhood is the different smells. It's a mix of Dominican street food, fish, laundry, fresh air, marijuana, and cigarettes. It mostly only smells like Dominican street food and fish west of Broadway. I live on Broadway but sometimes I go west of Broadway if I want to shop, get food, or ride the 1 train. My favorite things about Inwood are the parks, especially Fort Tryon Park. It's so peaceful there. It's just as nice as Central Park except it's smaller. It's not as generic and there are definitely not as many people there. I like it better. I can bring my friends there, do whatever I want, and no one bothers us. It's like my sanctuary where I chill out and enjoy the scenery. I used to go there every day last summer with my ex-boyfriend. We would chill out and drink beer and talk. I don't go there with him any more, but I still bring my friend Marcela from time to time. I plan to bring a lot of my friends there this summer to do the same.

Washington Heights, the neighborhood right below Inwood, in many respects is a lot like Inwood, but is missing one thing that Inwood has: integration. Although it's just as diverse and there are many different groups of people, it's very segregated there. All the Dominicans are east of Broadway. The yuppies all hang around the Starbucks west of Broadway, and the Jewish community is mostly over by the yeshiva. There is some integration, but the different groups mostly have their own places and for the most part keep to themselves. It might be about real estate; I don't know.

In Inwood though, the different social groups seem to come together. One generalization that I can make about the majority of the people in the neighborhood is that most people tend to be laid back. But, the food is better in Washington Heights. I definitely could not stay in Inwood for the rest of my life, but that's because I also couldn't stay anywhere forever. However, right now at this point in my life, I love living there.

WHEN I GET OFF THE A TRAIN

During the winter or the fall, it's usually dark by the time I exit the subway. When I get off the A train, the end of the staircase faces Inwood Park, the newsstand, and the Doo-op Deli (both stores are usually closed by this time). I turn the corner where the photo shop, nail salon, and Capital Diner all stand. If I get home before 9:30 p.m., Capital Diner is still open. Next up is the bus stop where I take the express bus in the morning. The bus stop is just a large pole with a square-shaped schedule attached. Next is the barbershop. The men who stand in front of the barbershop are not like most guys who stand in front of places in Inwood. They are not saying vulgar things at the women and girls who pass by. Next on the block is this new Papa John's Pizza that just opened, which bothers me because Inwood is not about chain stores and big corporations. Most of the companies in Inwood are family- or privately owned.

As I keep walking by, I pass the Dyckman farmhouse. The Dyckman farmhouse is this big white house in the middle of the block; it's a museum that houses antiques from the colonial period. When I finally get to my block, I usually stop at the corner store, Fidel's "Gourmet" Deli.

INTERVIEW WITH JOHN MAZZELLA, OWNER OF DOO-OP DELI

Have you ever lived in this neighborhood, besides having this shop?
No.

What made you decide to open up your deli in this neighborhood?
I used to serve this store. I used to deliver to it. I liked what I saw, and I decided to buy it! It was up for sale.

What did you like about it?
I loved the neighborhood. The neighborhood was dynamite back then.

Why?
It was a middle-class neighborhood. It was a little bit mixed, predominantly Irish and Jewish. That's what I wanted to go into. I had a deli before this in an Irish and Spanish neighborhood, and I liked it. I decided to come back to it.

What year did you open up the deli?
1976.

Do you notice what changed about the neighborhood?
We went from a predominantly Irish neighborhood to an 85 percent Dominican neighborhood. Now it's turning back to middle- to upper-class neighborhood.

Do you like the change?
Change is hard, especially when you're trying to please a lot of people. Change is very hard. But we'll adapt to it all as we go along.

PASTELITO ADVENTURES

It was mid-summer, 2007, about three weeks before I went to Spain. I was with my friends Kyle and Marcela.

I met Marcela during my freshman year at Talent Unlimited, a performing arts high school. She started speaking in some sort of Spanish accent. I didn't quite get it; she looked Asian. Then she told me she was half Japanese but was born and raised in Mexico. She had come to New York during the summer right before high school began. Apparently she was sort of famous in Mexico, like a child pop sensation or something of the sort. Marcela is one of the craziest people I have ever met in my entire life. She makes up stories all the time and has the most obscure outlook on life that I have ever heard. She's completely interesting, and that's what I love about her. I would hate to have boring friends; all of my friends have something strange and unique about them.

Kyle is the boyfriend of my friend Tatiana who I also met at Talent Unlimited. I met Kyle during that year but not until the end of it. I ended up becoming pretty good friends with him. He's a quiet guy from upstate, but when you get to know him, he's really funny and deep. Tatiana and he had just broken up a few days before this, and he was really upset.

I had one night of having the apartment all to myself. Marcela, Kyle, and I were just hanging around in the dark; Marcela and I were making a musical. We all eventually got really hungry. I was pretty much out of groceries, but it was two o'clock in the morning. What do you do at two o'clock in the morning in Inwood when nothing is open and you are really hungry? You go to the pastelito truck for pastelitos: small Cuban pastries with various fillings. Marcela decided to play dress up before we went on our little adventure to the pastelito truck. She put on this crazy long black and white skirt that my mom used to wear in the mid-'90s, and a big yellow jacket that had the Ranch 1 logo on the back. She tied a blue scarf around her head, put a hat over that, and wore star-shaped sunglasses and really ugly mustard-colored boots. She looked unbelievably ridiculous.

We went outside, looking around for an open pastelito truck. We walked down to Dyckman. Marcela was stumbling behind us trying to convince the world that she was the neighborhood crack head. Eventually, we reached a pastelito truck. There were a whole group of guys and one or two  girls in line getting their pastelitos. That was when Marcela really started to vent out. She started pointing to the meat that was on display in the window of the truck. "Pork's stomach." She pronounced what she was saying in this ridiculous overdone accent so that it sounded like "pork's stowmak." "It is the stowmak of the pork," she said, as she ecstatically pointed to the meat. All the Dominican men started laughing hysterically and talking about her in Spanish saying things like "Check out the crazy Asian woman," and other things along those lines. Of course, they had no way of knowing Marcela was actually Mexican and spoke fluent Spanish. So than she started saying "Estómago de un puerco," which means "pork's stomach" in Spanish. I was just standing there laughing my guts out.

Kyle found it pretty funny too; he was laughing. I don't think the man in the pastelito truck took us very seriously, and after about a half an hour of standing in front of the truck, we realized we weren't getting any pastelitos from there. Marcela then explained to everyone that she was an actress playing the role of a crazy person. Then we walked down to the next truck another avenue down. She started with the same act again, but this time it didn't last as long because we actually really wanted to get the pastelitos. We finally got what we came for. We bought two with chicken, two with cheese, and two with beef. We walked back to the apartment and ate a little on the way, laughing about what had just occurred. On the way back, we stumbled across some corner men who were saying vulgar things to try to catch my attention. Marcela started yapping at them, saying that she was my mother. We finally made our way back to my house, scarfed down the pastelitos, and fell right to sleep.

INTERVIEW WITH SHAMIE

My name is Shamie Cuthbert; I am twenty-six years old. Today is May 12, and I am at Grand Central Terminal, and I am with my sister, Noelle.

Where do you live exactly?
I live in Washington Heights, New York. I like the diversity of the neighborhood, definitely. I like the fact that there are people from within the country but from all sorts of states. As a parent and as a mother, I like the community factor of the neighborhood. I like that we can build a community in New York City where you don't feel as anonymous as you feel downtown.

And what don't you like about the neighborhood?

I don't like the evident segregation of economic disparity.

And how has the neighborhood changed since you first moved there?

It's definitely become more gentrified. It's improved as far as businesses are concerned. There are a lot more restaurants and stores and activities for children. It's become the sort of place to move to outside of the expensive area of New York, and it's thriving.

So, you see the gentrification as a good thing?

For selfish reasons, I see it as a good thing.

If you could change one thing about the neighborhood, what would it be?

Basically, I would change east of Broadway. It's still a little bit dangerous. There are halfway houses. It's very dirty in certain areas. There are kids outside playing with fire hydrants and throwing garbage on the streets. I feel that the gentrification is centered in one specific area. I would hope that it kind of spreads a little bit without shutting out an entire people. If the two communities on both sides of Broadway could come together and work with each other, it would be better than having two separate worlds. It's possible.

So how do you find Washington Heights and Inwood different?

My experience at Inwood is different because I don't know that many people. I don't actually feel that community, small-town, neighborhood feel that you feel in Washington Heights, because it's unfamiliar to me. Aesthetically, I find that Washington Heights is more visually appealing. I find that Inwood is still rough around the edges compared to Washington Heights.

So where did you grow up?

All over the place in Manhattan and Queens.

Which one was your favorite place to live, out of all the places?

72nd and Riverside where I lived when I was seven, eight, and nine. It was peaceful. It was at the edge of the Upper West Side. And I like the Upper West Side. I kind of see it as classic New York. It's just very, like, *Annie Hall*.

And how is it different than Washington Heights?

Money is the thing that sort of fuels the difference in New York City as far as neighborhoods are concerned. I mean, a neighborhood is sort of characterized by how much money there is and what people choose to do with that money.

What was the least favorite neighborhood you grew up in?

Woodhaven Boulevard, Rego Park. I hate that part of Queens. I just sort of see it as the epitome of mediocrity. I felt that it was a passionless place. There was nothing aesthetically pleasing about it. One of the greatest things about New York City is that it's a place for sensualists. You can look at something, and it's beautiful, and you smell beautiful food, and you hear music, and it's appealing to all your senses. I feel like in Queens, there was a dearth of beauty.

Interesting. And where did you live right before you moved to Washington Heights?

We lived in the Bronx, Parkchester. It was an experience. Definitely not visually appealing at all. Every building looked the same. I felt like I was in a prison. But the neighborhood really did have some benefits to it. It was a new experience for me. The neighborhood was primarily African American. I enjoyed living there, now that I'm looking back on it. Growing up in New York City as a non-African American, you're given the idea that all neighborhoods that are solely African American are just dangerous. Or you're

given this negative viewpoint. It wasn't like that at all. It was very friendly. It was also like a small town. It was set up by the same architect that built Stuyvesant Town. It was built so that children can walk around the entire area to school and home without having to cross any streets. So that was a nice foundation for a neighborhood.

Why did you decide to move to Washington Heights after leaving Parkchester?

Well, I had to move because our landlord was selling the apartment. And Washington Heights was pretty much the best option and the most doable option.

What was the most spiritually awakening moment of your life?

I don't feel like I've had it yet. I mean, I feel like everyone has small moments of spiritual awakenings, and they might not be realized until later on when you're reminded of them. I think spiritual awakening is a series of minor epiphanies.

Can you explain one of them?

That's a hard question. I guess when my son was born. *Spiritual* is a very open term for me. It's intellectual and emotional. It's all sort of interconnected. I would say when Jacob was born, the main thing that changed was that life became more simple. I felt like I knew what was important and what was not important.

FORT TRYON PARK

I live in New York City and have never lived anywhere else in my entire life. It's hard to find places where I can become connected to a more natural environment. There is always Central Park, but it's constantly flooded with tourists, yuppies, and junkies that never graduated from Strawberry Fields. Fort Tryon Park isn't as crowded. That's what's great about living near Fort Tryon.

Fort Tryon Park starts on 187th Street and goes all the way up to Dyckman and 200th Street. The entrance closest to where I live is on Dyckman. There is a small community garden on a little island across from the entrance. On Dyckman, there are two possibilities for entering the park. You can enter in the front where the playground is, or you can walk down the street and enter where the walking path lies. I usually enter where the walking path is, but I never go in alone, mainly because I'm afraid of getting raped. Ever since that Julliard student was raped and murdered in Inwood Park years ago, I never walk alone in the park.

I cannot recall a time where I felt more alive in my life than I did one brilliant day at Fort Tryon Park with my friend. It was as if I had the world in the palm of my hands; there was no way I would ever let it go. I remember everything from that moment – the feeling of the grass on the tips of my fingers, the way the air felt as we ran against it, the way he would look at me and then burst out laughing. We were two kids, and we had this park, and it was as if we had it all to ourselves. I giggled, and then we just fell onto our backs. It was as if I was stuck in this great moment I thought I would never become separated from. He wasn't laughing because something was funny. It was because he was happy. I knew that because I was too; it was exhilarating. I was sixteen at the time and it was his eighteenth birthday.

Fort Tryon Park is an amazing place, but I don't think I could ever re-live that day or feel the way I did then. Experiences are unique in that sense. They only come once and that's the beauty of it all.

I look around me, and it's still that stunning place it was before. Just the feeling of being around more than one tree at a time is still mind-altering for a city kid like me. However, the excitement is gone. Though this is not necessarily a bad thing. Now I am left feeling comfortable; I'm now used to this place. I sit on the bench and look at the contented emptiness around me. Someday, something will be exciting and new to me, but for now I'll embrace what has grown on me, my home.

Harlem, Manhattan
SOFIJA KULIKAUSKAS

MY REAL DESTINATION, HARLEM

I was born on March 9, 1992. I lived in Queens, New York, for about 10 years before I moved to my real destination, Harlem. I used to be a child of fairy tales; everything was supernatural. Now my eyes are opened wider. Living in Queens was just like living in Neverland with Peter Pan, but living in Harlem is the real deal. It's my real home. People always call it a "bad place," but in truth, it's reality. Living in Harlem changed my views about everything and developed who I was. I found style, culture, and rhythm. It made me tough, open minded, and curious. It showed me how to be real, how to be a person of honesty.

I've witnessed the good and bad of Harlem, but that just doesn't change my views of my neighborhood. I stand out a lot because of my skin color. People stereotype, which doesn't make me happy. They expect a white girl living in Harlem to be rich and scared. You can tell by my walk, talk, and style that I'm not close to fitting that category. Living in Harlem, I became this new person who just wanted to see everything about where I lived. Later, this caused me to get in trouble. As I developed slowly, I noticed that where I live, I shouldn't be open. It's better to just be a mysterious character. Now people see me on the streets and think, "That's the white girl who lives down the block, and she ain't like them other folks." I think I am one of a kind because I've embraced Harlem's culture into my own lifestyle and future.

FAMILY OF MINE

I came out of my mother, and she was my family because the rest of my family was hardly around in my childhood. My mother's family is all in Lithuania; she has two sisters, her parents, aunts, uncles, and my cousins. I consider her close friends here, who

I've known almost my whole life, to be family. On my father's side, I've only met my grandmother. She used to come to New York every year to live with us for long periods of time. In the last five years, her health needs have caused her to stay in Lithuania.

My family only consists of my mother and me. One man dropped out of my life: my father, who now lives in Queens with his own family. Soon Lye Lim is the father that I live with now. He is the reason I live in Harlem and have such a good life and a new, three-year-old sister. It can be a bit rocky, but I know I can come back to a warm home and a meal because of him and my mother.

Another part of my family is my older half brother, Kristijonas. He visits us every year. I hardly get to see him because he always comes to work and always brings his girlfriend, who is probably going to be my sister-in-law. When I see him, I make the best of it. I look up to him as my big, invincible brother. We don't have the type of friendship where we tell each other everything, but we have that sister-brother bond. Hopefully we'll get closer when he moves over here from Lithuania. We have different mothers but the same, unpredictable father.

My theory about my father is that he had my brother when he was too young. He had me when he was too busy, at his peak of his career, so he had no time for me. Now that his life is settled and he has his job, he is fine with his new three-year-old baby. My father is a small factor in my life. He mostly supports me through money or words. I can't ever forgive him for what he has done to impact my life, but I will always love him because he is my father, the man who tried to give me the world. He failed because he was

influenced by the wrong substance and never had time for me.

The family of mine consists of my mother, my stepfather, my sister, and me. Hopefully, it will stay that way through the good and bad. A good family has your back 24 hours a day, seven days a week, through holidays and summer breaks.

LIKE A NOMAD

After we left my father in Kew Gardens, we lived in Richmond Hill, Queens, in a small apartment above John's Ice Cream Parlor. When my mother got pregnant with Alex in 2002, we moved to Harlem, into my stepfather's new townhouse. We own the three apartments of the townhouse; we live in one and rent out the other two. When we moved here, we heard comments about the neighborhood because at that time it was a bit dangerous. Now it has improved a bit.

I was fascinated by where I lived because it was so different from Queens. Even though I miss my old neighborhood, like a nomad, I like to see something new. Usually in Queens, you are able to stay outside late playing Manhunt, Hide-and-Seek, kickball, tag, and all those games. In Harlem, things didn't seem that way. I hardly knew anyone; I was starting a new school, and I was minority in that 'hood. After about a year in Harlem, things changed. I knew a lot of people in the neighborhood and got used to the city life. I met so many new friends and went to all parts of Harlem and even to different parts of the city. My mother still makes comments about the neighborhood. Either the sidewalks are too cracked, or people throw garbage in her garden.

Some of my friends who live in Queens were a bit critical about where I lived and hardly ever came over to see me. So I hardly saw them, and we drifted apart from each other. The new friends I made in school, in Harlem, and around the city have lasted me a long time.

Harlem is a type of neighborhood where you see everyone outside with his or her friends, just chilling and talking out on the block. Everyone from the neighborhood is friendly to my family, and they always see me around, just walking to different places in my 'hood.

So far, my family and I are enjoying where we live because it has all the resources we need, and the trains and buses are close by. I don't have any problems living in Harlem. There are times when I wish I could live either more uptown or more downtown, but so far, I'm just in the middle.

INTERVIEW WITH FRANCINE RODGERS

I am going to be interviewing my mother, Francine Rodgers. How long have you been living in Harlem?
Five years.

And so far do you like it?
It's challenging. Harlem was always a famous place for violence and crime. It's not very diverse, and it's hard to be an outsider in a community where one kind of people live. Some African Americans have hard feelings towards whites.

Do you think the neighborhood changed after we moved here?
It did. There are more restaurants, more jazz clubs, and more diverse people. The rats are gone, almost. All these buildings were abandoned, so it was rat paradise. Every time you went outside, there were plenty of rats running around.

Where are your favorite places to go?

We used to go to Sylvia's, but it got too commercial. There are a few restaurants, like Mobay. Make My Cake is a good bakery. Shopping, I still do in New Jersey, Midtown, or Upper West Side. We don't have good supermarkets. We have lots of jazz places here. Everybody is invited. There's a very nice jazz association, which is 100 years old. Every Monday they have jazz jams, which I go to. I'm meeting people. There are a lot of old timers, good musicians and singers, and newcomers who want to try. My friend Sandy has jazz evenings from Thursday to Sunday.

Did you have any bad experiences in Harlem?

When I parked my car when I first moved, they smashed my windshield with a bat. Then they would call me crack head because white people used to come into the neighborhood for drugs. Cursing me out, giving me looks. Sometimes, we didn't even want to go out. So I said to myself: you live here, or you move out. So I decided to live here in Harlem, and see what I can do. I made some friends.

Can you tell me how you felt when there was a shooting right in front of our building?

I had just got inside the house. I came from work very late, like at one a.m.. As soon as I stepped in the house, I got some water, and I heard BOOM, BOOM! I went to the window and heard the girl screaming, so I called the police. One of my neighbors had already called, so the police were already there. I was very sad that two young people died. They were part of the gang. It's pretty sad. I come from a country where there weren't any racial issues. There, it was very interesting to have different people come. We admire dark skin. I think some

African Americans went from slavery to slavery within welfare. Seeing these young girls with kids, it's like not having your experience in life. It's harder to find out who you are or what you are going to do with your life. Having children when you are yourself a child is kind of sad. I hope it will change.

Now all of a sudden, you see two cops on every block. Do you know why they did that? Is it because new, white people are moving in, and they want to keep the neighborhood safe, just to make Harlem the new place to live for rich, white people? You see a lot of condos, new apartments, and renovated brownstones being built. Or do you think the government and the police opened their eyes and said, "We need some security in Harlem."

Of course they need more security because every day they find some house with the crack or people selling drugs. They're trying to clean it out. A lot of people who are moving in are not just white. There are plenty of African Americans who are successful, who are Harvard graduated, who are making good money, and they are moving here too. But they cannot get along together. It's not just me who's been called names. Africans look at the African Americans who are doing nothing. They are working three jobs, and they want a better life.

Before you moved to Harlem, where else did you move?

Queens, Queens, Queens.

And what places did you live in Queens?

Oh God, first Corona. A little room, with ninety-degree heat.

We were staying in an attic?

No it was like, first floor. And then we moved to another house. It was one room in a house with maybe seven or eight rooms, with different people living in them – all immigrants from Eastern Europe.

Tell me about before you moved to America. What was it like living in Lithuania?

Pretty good. I had a good life. I had a good job. I enjoyed what I did. I didn't come here for anything. I thought I was coming for vacation. And then my ex-husband, your father, decided not to go back. So I said, okay, let's try a challenge. And it was interesting. Not knowing the language. I brought only one pair of jeans, a pair of shoes. It took me a long time to get another pair of shoes. We didn't have money. We didn't have jobs. We didn't have papers. I started babysitting, working as a companion, and cleaning. I remember I bought my first pair of shoes from a very nice store on Delancey for five dollars. I wore them until nothing was left.

Do you think you would ever go back to Lithuania?
I don't think so. Lithuania is too small a country for me. I probably would be in South Africa with the rest of my friends. I cannot afford it right now, but I would like to visit my friends.

Are you happy living here?
If my family is all right, everything is okay. I'm happy, anyway. You cannot get happiness outside. You could get temporary happiness, but you have to have happiness within yourself.

I'm not happy here. I mean, I like it, but I would prefer to live somewhere a little more uptown, a little more downtown, or midtown. But this block, I don't know. I see the same people every day, the same stories every single day. Nothing's really changing except for a few new people, but they're not talking to us. The new white people who moved in, they're not even speaking to us. Usually in those neighborhoods, they would come and bring a pie. Like, "Hey, new neighbors!" Since we moved a lot, I feel like a nomad. I don't want to live here until I'm eighteen.
You have a long life ahead.

What if I die?
If you die, you're going to have the whole universe.

Do you have any last words you want to say?

Make yourselves happy. Study hard, explore, and don't get pregnant. Before you decide to have children or marry, you have to know who you are and what you want. You have to experience things. Travel. Life is not just four walls, and a house is not a home. Do extra work, read more books, and open your minds.

STEREOTYPES AND RACISM

My 'hood has its ups and downs. The police system keeps us safe, but the police have an ugly side to their law. I have witnessed their dark side directed towards some of my friends in my 'hood. I'd heard they're known to be racist or judgmental towards teenagers. There was one night I found out those rumors were true.

It was an active Tuesday night. My friends Tomas, Yahie, and Kevin had bought flavored Smirnoffs and a Budweiser from the store. We were walking down the block of 146th and Amsterdam where Tomas lives. This is one of my favorite hangouts. We saw a NYPD van across the street with the lights all around, and we kept looking back. Tomas was on a bike, and he kept telling us to stop looking back because we looked suspicious, and they might notice us. We didn't listen to him and just laughed and walked. Tomas rode away, and we went on with our business.

Kevin told Yahie, "Give it to me," or "Pass it." He meant the drink. I didn't even notice this black car rolling right next to us, holding two white guys and one Black guy who were looking at us. They didn't seem like they were part of the neighborhood, and right away I knew they were cops.

They stopped and said, "Can we talk to you for a minute?" I started to walk a little bit faster, but right before I knew it, they came out and told Kevin to stand against the wall.

I didn't know what to do, so I just walked, frightened, holding a Smirnoff bottle against my chest. I took out my cell phone and automatically pretended to call my mom. I walked a little further, praying to God they wouldn't tell me to stop, and they didn't. I was surprised. I walked a little further away from them, toward the end of the block, rested my bottle near a car on the ground, and walked back.

I saw one of the white cops searching Kevin all over and taking things out of his pockets. Yahie just stood there with the black bag with the drinks looking scared out of his mind. I stood there, upset that they were just checking Kevin and not Yahie or me. I asked, "Why are you just checking him? We were with him."

The other white cop looked at me and said, "Can you just step back." I didn't move.

"Please go over there until we've finished."

I replied, "No, that's not right." I didn't move, just crossed my arms in front of my chest and looked him dead in the eye. He just turned back around and waited for the other cop to finish checking Kevin.

The Black cop turned to Yahie and started to just check him. He took the bag and said, "It's ok. Just drink your beer." The white cop who checked Kevin said he was clear, and he was just checking if he had any possession of drugs. They apologized and went back into the car while I just gave them a dirty look. It made me feel so disgusted that what I witnessed was truth. In the end we just laughed about it, but we kept saying how it was wrong for them to just check Kevin since he was Black and not Yahie and me just because we were light skinned. I asked Kevin, "Did that ever happen to you before?" and his reply was, "Yeah, many times."

Cops in my neighborhood do that a lot on my block, 133rd Street, to most of the guys on the corner. They choose the most "ghetto"-looking guys and check them, especially because of their color. I don't have anything against cops, but what they do to my neighborhood and to the people in it just is so sad. It should change as soon as possible.

BOYS IN THE 'HOOD

Around my neighborhood, you will always find guys on the corner. They're usually chilling and socializing with one another, standing on the corner by the deli. In the winter, you usually see them wearing big coats by Marmot, North Face, Pelle Pelle, and the leather ones, too. They wear baggy jeans with Nike boots, Air Nikes, Jordans, etc.. Any day that I walk by them, you would hear them saying "Ayo ma, come ova here lemme talk to you for a minute, lemme getcha numba, you so sexy." They always say "Hey snow bunny, snowflake, vanilla Dutch, white chocolate," or something having to do with how I look.

In the morning, you can walk down those blocks and not see anyone. They are nocturnal – from seven a.m. to two p.m., there is no one on those corners, just parked cars. Once it hits two-thirty or three p.m., you see them come out, rowdy and making a lot of commotion. If someone other than a girl walks by them, they make some funny comments and say something negative. They make fun of what that person is wearing, how he looks, and possibly who he is with.

Each time I pass them, I always have to look at my phone, be on the phone, or keep looking straight ahead, so I don't have to be hollered at. I get a bit nervous or annoyed when it comes to walking home at night. They always say something to me like "Take me home with you." I get tired of constantly getting talked about and called to like I'm a dog. It pisses me off, and that causes me to curse them out. Some are cute, but we all know what they want from us ladies.

Some around my block know me and are known to be cool; they mind their business. They all are trying to survive and hustle hard in different ways, legal or illegal. It makes me feel sad because I know some of them are not going to go anywhere. Those faces I see today – I may see them again on that same corner in a few years. There is a chance that they won't be there for different reasons. Some make it, some don't, – either the hard way or the easy way.

BACK AT YA, BOYS

Pssst!!!!

Stud muffin

Hey fella!

What's up sexy?

Hmmm. . .

He's so fresh

Ay papi chulo

Yo cutie!!

Ayo sexi!

DAMN!

What a stud!

Que guapo papi

He's a hottie!

What a hunk.

146TH STREET FAMILY

The boys in my 'hood that I know on 146th Street don't stand on the corner as part of their daily life. They hang out at the store where one of my friends works or near the post office by their buildings. They just are all together having fun, talking, and playing around.

I constantly went to that block to see my cousins and friends and met these boys through them. We all became cool and stayed in touch. Every time I'm with them, I bet people think I am messing around with them, but that's not even the case because they're like a family to me. The whole block is like one family, but people stick to who they know. If someone from another block tries to start something on my friends' block – their territory– they have each other's back.

I try to look out for these boys I know on 146th Street. I lecture them a lot about not fighting or getting involved in stupid acts. There was one night when I saw one of the boys from the block on 145th with some of his friends. A few guys from another block surrounded him, and I heard one of my boys saying, "You called me pussy?" The other replied, "Yea, I called you pussy, and what?" and then punched him in the jaw. It was a big fight, going back and forth. I got so upset, I went to 146th and started talking to the guys and telling them how I felt that it was stupid to fight. They probably didn't pay any mind to what I had to say because they all are stubborn boys and were getting ready to fight once again. It got late and really cold so I went home. The next time I saw them they told me they didn't fight.

There are also girls from the block who chill with some of the guys. All the parents know each other also. Some girls are judged wrongly and are known to be "sluts" – as in, they mess with more then one guy on the block. I know some of the girls on the block, and they are cool. But there are a few that always try to start some kind of challenge about who was with which guy first. I just laugh and shrug because I have nothing to worry about. The boys all know we are like a family.

I want to see them get out of this neighborhood and/or move on to a good life. I love them a lot, and they are characters. I wouldn't want to see their lives go to waste. I always hope for the best for them because I know they have chances to make a change. Only the strong can do it and survive. Others are just lazy or not willing to change. Hopefully, things will be a bit better for them and their community.

Anyone can be misrepresented, standing on the corner as though he is a drug dealer of some kind. I remember seeing people from my old school on those corners, always going to the "chicken spot," chilling with their friends, having fun, laughing, and talking. Guys on the corner cause trouble and can cause a commotion between one another. It can get heated. Then someone gets hurt or dies. You see them on that corner now, but maybe in a day, maybe in a week, or in a few years, you probably won't see their face again.

INTERVIEW WITH EUGENE

My name is Eugene. I'm eighteen years old. Today's date is February the 28, 2008. The location is Grand Central Terminal StoryCorps Booth, and my relationship to my interview partner is friendship.

So where do you live?
I live in the Upper West Side, also known as Hamilton Heights in Harlem. 145th Street and Amsterdam. It's pretty good.

Why do you like it?
I have a very diverse community. We have Hispanic, Chinese, Japanese, Black, Italian, and some people I forgot to count right now. We also have Lithuanians, and we have British, French, and all sorts of people.

I was born in downtown Manhattan and lived in Harlem my whole life. I go to school. I'm an actor and a model. I also work for the New York City Department of Health, which is a great job. I work for the disease intervention program. We work with STD information. We also work with the New York information hotline, 311, and we send educational postcards and films to schools. We send out condoms and everything else for teenagers to be aware of. I'm one of the few teens that work for the Department of Health. I was transferred from disease control. I worked for a clinic over on 128th Street, and it wasn't that big of a transition because I still dealt with STDs and flu shots. I think of it as saving the world. I love helping people. We just got a whole box of condoms in the school. They don't know I'm behind that, but it feels pretty good.

Do you think you're helping your neighborhood by doing that, too?

Yeah. Because of all the things that are going on in the world now and what's going on in Harlem with the rate of HIV, AIDS, STDs, I actually feel that I'm helping because condoms can prevent most of that. We send out brochures to tell people, mostly teenagers, to watch out.

Teeners.

Yeah teeners. Yeah we tell teenagers to watch out, watch what they're doing, and slow down on the sex drive.

[StoryCorps Interviewer]: When did you two meet for the first time?

The girls always know the whole story, while the guys don't really give details.

My friend, Joselito, was going through a whole bunch of people on his MySpace, and he goes to Eugene. And then, I'm like, "Oh, okay." A few years later, I'm at a movie set.

Yeah, we were at a movie set for a certain film.

Yeah, okay. And I was like, "I seen you before, but I forgot who you are." And then I asked him where he lived, and my cousin lives a building away from him. So we exchanged numbers. Then about six months later we actually talked because I saw him coming down my cousin's block –

Yeah that was three times in a row for a week.

That was twice. And then, he was like, "Oh, you remember my name?" because his name is so weird but so common. I was like, "'It's Eugene," and he was like, "Yeah." And so I guess we just talked on MySpace, and then we became friends. When we

spoke, he was a model, and I was just wondering, *how do you live here?* Then we met up on 125th Street. But anyways, I guess he's an actor and model, and he's all creative and smart. He's a good person. He's not like a regular guy. He'll be like, "No, you got to fix this, that," and he makes fun of you. I guess it's his character that I like. And I like his neighborhood.

How is your neighborhood? How did it affect you? Did it build you up?

What affected me most about where I live is pretty much my family. Both of my parents grew up in New York, and they had this whole insight on what goes on in New York City. They lived around 140th in Harlem. So while I was growing up, all I heard was, "You should be safe." Things used to go on in Harlem sometimes. But actually, it's not that bad.

Exactly.

Parents always give you the bigger picture of everything, so you do not get hurt or anything from outside. It actually helped me become more mature at a young age. Also, there were other people that grew up in Harlem who are actually famous now. I feel that as I get more into acting, I can actually be one of those people that grew up in Harlem, from New York City, who are on the silver screen one day. That sounds good. Hey, I love what I do.

You live in a great place. How about you explain where you live? She lives in, like, the nicest place in Harlem.

I live on 133rd Street and Lenox in a brownstone. It's about the family. I don't like staying in that house all the time because I feel lonely, and there's nobody there. So I go outside and roam the streets. I was born in Queens. I can just say I was born there because I was more or less raised in Harlem. As you said, it made me more mature at a young age. I had to go through all the racist comments and all the problems because I was a female, with all the guys trying to holler at me and stuff. I got tired of everybody calling me Snowflake and Snow Bunny and etc., etc., etc.. Let's not get into that. I just got tough. I just didn't want to take any more b.s. from all this. In the beginning it would hurt me when people said racist comments, but now – *okay, you're ignorant. Get over yourself. Stop!*

Yeah, we should switch lives because she actually lives in a place I want to buy. I'm actually thinking about buying the whole block, which would be nice.

[StoryCorps Interviewer] I was just curious. It's 2008; are your friends and family accepting and supportive of the fact that you guys are really close friends?

My mom knows him. His mom sort of, kind of, knows me. My parents like him.

Yeah, I talk to my parents about her. There's nothing really to say. Pretty much, my family is colorblind. We're all mixed – a whole bunch of stuff. But to accept a person is actually, it's not out there. It's just like, you're a really nice person, and you got to be welcome to enjoy our company.

That's how my mother feels too. They see you as a person, not as a color. It's so ignorant to see somebody by color. You can't say you can't see color because you still see color. But you have to notice what kind of person he or she is. You just can't judge exactly – like saying you can't judge a book by its cover. See what's on the inside first. I guess that's how we are.

[StoryCorps Interviewer] Can you each say one thing that you are looking forward to about growing older?

I want to change people's views on other people, especially America's views, because it's a very capitalist country. I want to be a lot of things. I want to help people with their problems, go into sociology or anthropology. I'm fascinated by people and what they think. It's part of becoming a revolutionary woman. I stand for people's rights, and peace, and changing the world. I'm a part of the A.N.S.W.E.R. [Act Now to Stop War and End Racism] Coalition. I want to try something out. Try something different.

You're such a small person, and you want to change the world. When I found that out, I was like, wow. Good luck with that. That's all I can say because I never thought that I would do anything like that. I just want to make money. I got to be honest. I like making people feel good, but it's totally different from her because her biggest thing is that she wants to help people in every way. She wants to dedicate her life to doing it.

[StoryCorps Interviewer] Could you describe the image of a revolutionary woman?

A person who gives speeches and uses fierce words to attack people's wrong decisions. I just want to educate people. I know there are always going to be ignorant people, but I just really want to change that. I'd like to see a bigger picture since I have such an open mind. I really want people to look outside the box. Revolutionary women, like many anarchists, like Lucy Parsons, are trying to change the world.

Do you think you're going to live in your neighborhood for the rest of your life, or do you plan on moving?
I plan on moving. If I stay in New York City, I would get a condo in midtown Manhattan. The only thing that would bring me back to Harlem is that I want to buy the building my family lives in.

Sounds good to me. Let's go Harlem!

Upper West Side, Manhattan
FAITH HARRIS

NO COOKIES AND MILK

My name is Faith, but everyone and their mama calls me Faye. I was born June 30, 1991, in Beth Israel Hospital at nine eighteen p.m. I reside on the Upper West Side and have been there for the past sixteen years. I live with my mother, Jean Maria Harris, who has lived in our building for over thirty years. I call her one of the old timers in the neighborhood. She moved to the Upper West Side with my grandmother Lillian Harris in the 1960s. After my grandmother passed away, my mom had the apartment to herself, and, years later, had me. I wouldn't trade living here for anywhere else in the world.

All 16 years of my life, I've found my neighborhood pretty much welcoming. I'm not going to lie and say everybody stands around waiting for the fresh meat to come, or that we have cookies and milk to greet everybody, but we smile and say "Hi!" There are a few areas that aren't that welcoming. The best advice I can give is this: if you aren't comfortable in a certain environment, and you feel unsafe, then avoid it. Speaking from my perspective, everybody in my crew is welcoming. You can hang out with the crew you click with, otherwise you're screwed.

Everyone knows each other. You would be surprised who is friends with each other or related to each other in some sort of way. To this day, I'm still shocked by who knows whom in my neighborhood. News travels fast, very fast. Give it a couple of hours or a day, and everyone will know your business.

The reason for this is that everyone knows everyone, and there are some hangout spots just made for gossiping. When there's nothing better to do, that's when gossip comes in. Everyone just shares everyone's business. Trust me, I've been there. I've sat with people who talk about people's personal lives all day.

It probably sounds like I'm bashing my neighborhood, but there's always an up and a down side to everything. I would have to say, of all my experiences my neighborhood, making friends is the best. If you come off in a positive way, you are bound to make a few friends. Hopefully, then a bunch turns into a whole crew. I've made so many close friends that I can count on anytime I need them.

People who are not from here think it's a nice, quiet neighborhood where all the middle-class white folks live. In reality that's not what my neighborhood is all about. The African Americans, Hispanics, Caucasian, and Asian folks all come together. My neighborhood is diverse in ethnicity and in economic classes. On 100th and Amsterdam you might see the Douglass Projects where mostly the middle- and working-class Black and Latino families live. Down the block to another avenue, you see condos where all the wealthy Caucasian families live.

The place where people live doesn't stop them from getting together. I have a friend named Nick who comes from a wealthy home, and we are good friends. I mean, I've gotten those looks like, "What are you doing with him? You guys are complete opposites." I honestly don't care what people think about my choice of friends. Appearance doesn't affect the way I think of a person. I have many friends who don't have my same background, but it doesn't matter to me. As a child I was opened up to diversity at school, at summer camps, and in my own neighborhood. I never really judge anybody by skin color or background.

I think all neighborhoods should be diverse. It's good to open up to customs or cultures you are not used to. Diversity gives people the opportunity to be prepared for the real world. Being in a diverse environment expands your mind as a thinker. I think all the different types of people keep my neighborhood running, each and every day. There are three people who aren't what you think, and in some type of weird way, they stand out to me.

PHONE BOOTH LADY

I gave her the nickname Phone Booth Lady just last year because she always stands at the exact same phone booth on 94th and Amsterdam, in front of Budam's corner deli, whenever she is around the neighborhood. Bum Lady is what my friend Taj and I used to call her, but then we stopped because it was mean. The way she sets up the phone booth, you would think she stays there for a while. Usually you hear her mini radio. She loves to listen to Reggaeton or R&B, and dances to it all day, sometimes. She dances salsa when any type of Spanish music comes on. She just moves with the beat when R&B plays. Usually there's food from the deli she buys. She doesn't ask for money so I'm guessing people just give it to her. Sometimes you can catch her cursing at people or talking about her life experiences.

The first time I noticed her was when she was cursing at some random guy for no reason at all. It's funny because she once had a normal life. My close friend Isa's mother went to JFK High School with Phone Booth Lady. You would never think that. If you were to see her, it would look as if she's been homeless her entire life. Most people don't pay attention to her because she stays on the corner and talks mess. If people do pay attention, they just laugh and keep going.

One day I heard something she said, which I will never forget. She said she felt like a punk about crying when she was being raped in a park. Something told me she wasn't lying, and this was no story. At times I wish I could help her and provide her with what she needs because I feel bad about what she has gone through. I am curious about a daughter of hers that she has mentioned.

One time when I was coming home from school, I saw her in the subway station. I was curious about how she got there, but she was headed uptown. She sometimes disappears for a week or two. Maybe she has family up in Harlem.

GOD'S SAVIOR GUY

The second person who stands out to me is this guy who prays to Jesus on the street, from 96th to 106th. He's the type of guy you would think was crazy because of his long black jacket, the Bible he always carries in his left hand, and the fact that he is yelling and preaching all the time. From miles away, all you have to hear is "Bless you, bless you," and you already know who it is.

I never understood why he did what he did. I just thought it was because he loved the Bible so much and caught the Holy Ghost fever, but that was nowhere near why he is preaching himself to death. My friend Luis who is 20 years old had a conversation with him. The reason he goes around with his Bible, yelling, is because he claims he died, was reborn, and is thankful each and every day he lives. I thought that was just creepy. It's also really interesting. Ever since I discovered his story I tend to listen to every word he preaches. I discovered his words helped me a lot, which is kind of cool. I carry his words with me because they calm me down and help me with issues in my life. I can't believe I ignored him, and then that he was actually helpful.

JESUS

The last guy who stands out to me, Isa and I call Jesus because he claims he is Jesus all the time. It all started when Isa and I were eating at the Chinese restaurant. He got into an argument with the workers, and he said, "F*** you, I'm Jesus." To this day we call him Jesus. He always starts problems at the deli or the Chinese restaurant, curses at the workers, and then says he is Jesus. It's funny because I don't think Jesus would curse at workers. That guy just has mental problems. He does look like an African-American version of Jesus, though; I'll give him that much.

It's a random combination of people in my neighborhood. But I've learned you shouldn't judge people until you have heard what they say. Or just don't judge them at all because you never know what they went through or are going through.

HOTDOGS AND SUNKIST

I have some fun memories and some sad ones that are about my father and growing up in my neighborhood. A lot of memories take place in Central Park. Being so young and active, I enjoyed going to this one park located on 96th Street and Central Park West. It was my favorite park as a toddler when I needed somewhere to take out all my uncontainable energy. Rudin Playground was the place.

I usually sat anxiously on my bed waiting for my father to come and pick me up to take me there. My heart jumped when I heard the bell ring. My father walked into my house. I don't remember running so fast any other time in my life. I leapt into my father's arms while he gave me a big hug and kiss. Then he'd ask if I was ready to go.

My father always put me on his shoulders with my feet dangling across his chest. He was six foot, five inches, so it felt like I was on top of the world. The wind made my braids fly all over the place. I felt like I was riding a giraffe, and everyone was an ant. It seemed as if I were in a different world where the biggest things seemed small.

We had a tradition. Before we even stepped into the park, we had to get hot dogs and two cans of Sunkist soda (his favorite) from the street vendor who always stood on 96th across from the park. Sometimes he wouldn't charge my father for my hot dog because of how cute he thought I was. He would have a five-minute chat with my father about how things were. After they were done talking, I would tug on my father's shirt. I would rush him to the park because I was getting hungry just looking at my hot dog.

* * *

After my father's death six years ago, I stopped buying hot dogs from the vendor for a while. I just felt a bit weird going back to him without my father. I felt like that was our thing, and it wouldn't be our thing anymore if I bought hot dogs without him. To this day "the hot dog man," as I like to call him, is still there selling hot dogs and bringing smiles to people's faces. I always thought it was strange that for so many years I'd been buying hot dogs from this same guy over and over and never asked him his name. Now, every time I buy a hot dog from him I always raise it up to the sky and say, "This is for you, daddy."

* * *

"Don't forget to keep your legs straight," my father would shout as I soared through the air on the swings, pretending to be a witch on a broomstick.

There were times when I would go on the swings and wonder why I wasn't going as high as everyone else. I got so jealous of all the other kids who could touch a tree branch while swinging, when all I could touch was the cement with my toes. "Practice makes perfect," my father always used to say. I was never a quitter when it came to the swings. From the time the sun came up, to when the sun went down, I was glued to the swings like white on rice. One day, I was so excited because without my father pushing me, I was able to swing high. Touching the tree branch was the best thing that happened to me. After that moment, I felt like anything was possible.

After being exhausted from swinging on the swings and running around on the jungle gym, usually it would be close to dinnertime. From Rudin Playground, my father and I would go to a Chinese restaurant, now a Sushi restaurant, on 93rd and Amsterdam.

The people who worked there knew us pretty well. We also had a usual take-out order there. Chicken with broccoli (or just BBQ chicken, depending on how we felt), a large order of white rice, and two cans of Sunkist. Being an observant child, I used to study the restaurant: every wall, the ceiling, the cooks, and other customers' food. I remember the tables, the red booths, and Chinese decorations hanging up on the walls and ceiling. There was a red and gold, frightening dragon hanging from the ceiling, and I would always be scared of it as I came into the restaurant. Once the food came, I would stand on the seat in the booth and climb on my father's shoulders once again as we crossed the street and carried the food home.

Usually after eating I wanted to spend time with my father. We would play a board game or watch TV together before he left to go to back home, unless he decided to sleep over for the night. Jumping Monkeys was our favorite game. The player with the most bananas wins the game. I always won. Maybe he'd win one out of three games. After the third round my eyes would force themselves shut. Sometimes my father would talk me to sleep or read a story to me with my mother.

"Goodnight Daddy. Goodnight Mommy. Hope to see you soon," I would whisper.

JULIUS BURKE

My father, Julius Burke, was barely in my life before he passed away. He would be in and out most of the time, or he was just never there at all. He grew up down south in Savannah, Georgia with three sisters and two brothers, then moved to New York (Queens) where he met my mother. He also fought in one of the famous wars in American history: the Vietnam War. I remember as a child he showed me the scar on his right leg from getting shot while fighting in battle.

I had a special nickname when I was born. My father's side of the family called me "miracle child." After my father fought in the Vietnam War, the doctors said he wouldn't be able to have children because of chemicals used in the war. Who knew that many years afterwards, he would be the father of two children: my half brother Gerald and me?

When I turn eighteen, I want to get a tattoo dedicated to him. Even though he passed, and we can't see each other physically, his presence will always be with me. The following story is dedicated to him.

It was a Sunday evening in March, 2002, filled with no worries and no negative energy. I was at my friend Nayo's house joking around with her like we normally did on the weekends. Nayo's mom got a phone call from my mother asking her to take me home immediately.

When I got home, my heart dropped as my mother escorted me to my room and told me to sit on my bed. As I saw the expression on her face and the way she looked into my eyes, I knew that whatever she was about to tell me wasn't good. My heart started aching, my head started spinning, and I felt like I wanted to throw up. Silence filled my room for five to ten minutes. Then, when my mother was finally able to collect herself, she said, "I got to tell you something." I looked up from the floor; my eyes met hers. "Your father passed away from a heart attack."

I was in shock. I didn't know whether to cry and be upset or to just hold everything in and be strong. I just sat there not knowing what to think, but I did know one thing. This would affect my life and my heart forever. Even though my father and I didn't connect with each other like we should've, I still knew this would change me in all ways possible.

Now that he has passed, I will never be able to see him again. Only pictures and faded memories can bring him back in spirit. Who's going to interrogate that one special guy I bring home to introduce to my mom, or walk me down the aisle when I get married? All these questions started forming in my mind as I wondered who would fill his position in my life. For Father's Day he was never there, and the simple fact that he wouldn't be there with me now made me even sadder. At least before, there was a small ounce of hope that he would show up.

My mom gave me a hug and a kiss and told me if I needed anything she'd be in the living room. I still sat in my bed with tears rolling down my cheeks. I could taste the salt from the tears in my mouth. I came to the living room, and Nayo's mom gave me a big hug. It was one of those "I'm sorry for your loss and I will always be there for you" type of hugs. I sat in the living room, watched TV for a couple of minutes, and then decided to go to sleep with a part of my heart missing.

NOT *GILMORE GIRLS*

For seventeen years – my lifetime – I've lived with my role model and my idol: my mother. My mother has had a major impact on my life. Jean Harris was born and raised in New York City. She lived in Brooklyn but really grew up in Harlem on 144th between Seventh and Eighth Avenue with her aunt (my great aunt), Eleanor Harris, and our cousins. When my grandmother, Lillian Harris, passed away, my mother was in her twenties. That's when she started living on her own on the Upper West Side.

She was diagnosed with multiple sclerosis after she gave birth to me. As a child living with a parent with MS, you learn how to mature faster. When I was between the ages of nine and 10, there would be nights when my mom would fall to the floor in the middle of the night and stay there for hours. Her legs could give out, whether she was walking down the street or just getting up in the middle of the night to use the bathroom. It was frightening to wake up to find my mother on the floor. Sometimes, she was sleeping because she had been on the floor for so many hours, waiting for me to get up because she hadn't been able to get my attention. It was a struggle at times because she depended on me, and I could only do so much. Back then, I wasn't strong enough to help her get up myself, so I would have to call 911 or neighbors we were close to, so they could help her get back up. Sometimes, I was scared that one day my mom would fall so hard she wouldn't wake up. But God has been with her and hasn't let that happen.

Living with my mother inspires me a lot. I look up to her because she keeps me on my toes and does everything she can to make sure I'm happy. Our relationship isn't a *Gilmore Girls*, perfect relationship. We have our ups and downs but we get through them at the end of the day. She's played a father and mother role in my life, and I couldn't ask for anything better. She spoils me, which I love! She wants to make sure I get opportunities that she never had. I've traveled and seen things that some 30 year olds have never seen. I thank my mother for that because she's made me an open-minded person. At times, I don't realize how much of an amazing woman she is.

Without her, I don't know what I would do. She's super awesome. She's the greatest! I love you, Mommy!

RED DRAGON

I must say that a lot of people have shaped who I am today, but there's one female role model besides my mother whose spirit is with me all the time. It's my Aunt Dee. She isn't blood related to me, but she showed me you don't have to be blood to be family. She's just amazing, and I feel sorry for anyone who doesn't have an Aunt Dee like I do. I learn different life lessons from her when we're driving in her red Jeep Liberty or, as she likes to call it, her Red Dragon. I like watching her whip up her one-of-a-kind delicious mashed potatoes. She's always there when I need her, and vice versa. It's unbelievable, when you're a teenage girl, to have a best friend in her 50's. I have two: my mom and my Aunt Dee.

INTERVIEW WITH AUNT DEE

My name is Faith, and I'm sixteen. Today is March 6, 2008. I'm in the Grand Central Terminal in the StoryCorps Booth, and I'm interviewing my Aunt Dee.
My name is Dejah Lynch, "Dee." I am 53.

What's your occupation?
I'm a special-education educator.

How many years have you been teaching?
I have technically been teaching for three years, but I've been working with young people

for over forty. I'm am currently teaching the eighth grade at Fannie Lou Hamer Middle School in the South Bronx. I have about 25 students in a class.

Where do you reside in New York City?

I live in Manhattan, on the Upper West Side on 97th Street. I grew up in Harlem on 116th and Seventh Avenue (prior to it becoming Adam Clayton Powell Boulevard). I did not move directly to the Upper West Side from 116th. I lived in numerous places. I lived in Brooklyn. I shared an apartment in Spike Lee's father's brownstone before Spike Lee got famous. I lived in Queens. I lived in East Harlem. I also lived up on 151st. It was pretty intense. A lot of gangs. A lot of drugs. It wasn't really a safe neighborhood, although I felt fine living up there. Nice apartment– really big: four bedrooms. I could not find that now for the price I was paying then. I wanted to come down on the West Side because it is easier to get around the city. It's centrally located.

You said you lived in Spike Lee's brownstone. Did you know him personally?

Yes, I met Spike. That's when he was attending NYU, and he was doing his first film. I think it was *Joe's Barbershop* [*Joe's Bed-Stuy Barbershop: We Cut Heads*]. I used to talk to his father, who's a musician. I got the apartment because, at that time, I was working as a paralegal in Bed-Stuy for an attorney, whose name I would rather not mention. I was also going to Brooklyn College. It made more sense for me to live in Brooklyn than

to live in Manhattan, so I rented from Spike's dad for about a year. It was a brownstone with a really nice apartment.

How did it feel to live where there are a lot of gangs?

When I was growing up on 116th Street, heroin was number one. My neighborhood was the hot spot in the whole country for heroin. Living on 116th Street was not a big transition because I was accustomed to living in a very rough neighborhood. I was just not comfortable with a lot of gang activity.

Who do you live with now?

I live with my daughter, Nayo, and I have a kitten named Brooklyn.

How do you like your neighborhood now?

I like it because it's pretty mixed. You have not just different ethnicities, but also people who have different professions. There is a really wide variety in salaries. You have homeless people, and you have people making mega bucks. I've been there for 19 years. I moved there two years before I had Nayo, and she is 17.

How does it feel to look back at the neighborhood 17 years ago and to look at it now? Do you notice anything different?

When I first moved to 97th Street, it was not as congested. A lot of new buildings are going up now. We're right in the middle of gentrification. It's changing tremendously. People like me who are middle class are pretty concerned about where to live because we're very slowly being pushed out of the neighborhood. It's very obvious that New York is going from a place where you could sustain yourself to a place where you have to be really, really rich or really, really broke. It's really scary because you don't really know what's going to happen. If you don't own your own apartment or house, you really need to be concerned. So, I'm concerned because I don't own anything yet.

Where do you think the neighborhood is going to go in 10 years?

If it keeps going the way it's going, it's going to be more of what's happening now. For people just like me, working professionals who don't make over 100 grand, it's going to be hard. I'm concerned that they are slowly going to push us out, and where are we going to go?

Living in the neighborhood for so long, do you have any funny or sad stories to tell?
Well, the saddest story I can think of, you might remember. A young girl, about 13, committed suicide in my building about four years ago. Somehow, she was able to get on the roof. She had an argument with her mother and got really upset and jumped off the roof. I heard her when she fell. I didn't know what it was but we heard this big thump and a lot of noise. That was horrific. I have a child not too much older than the girl who committed suicide, so it was very traumatic for me. It really started me thinking. What would propel a young person to feel so hopeless that the only way to resolve her situation is to take her own life? It's pretty tragic.

Here's a funny story. One night, I was standing in front of the building, and some jazz musicians passed by. I didn't expect to see them. It was a nice surprise. They pulled out their saxophones and just started blowing right there on the corner because jazz musicians do crazy things like that sometimes. Just starting to rip. That was cool.

What are some of the hotspots in the neighborhood where you like to go?
I like to hang out in Harlem. If I hang out in the neighborhood, I go to a little Italian restaurant on 91st Street. I know the owner; he's really nice, very friendly. The food is great; the prices are reasonable. It has a nice atmosphere. That restaurant has lasted more than any other, so he's doing something right. You know, we like to go to Tex-Mex every now and then.

Yeah, I also like the Italian restaurant with the virgin Shirley Temples.
I'm sure you do.

Where do you like to shop?
Okay, this is bad. I don't like to shop in the neighborhood because it's kind of expensive.

We go down on Sixth Avenue between 16th Street and 21st Street because there are a lot of shops there. You have TJ Max, Old Navy, and Burlington, and then there are a lot of small shops. Plus, you know how much I love books. There are bookstores down there, too. It's pretty festive. I like to go to food shopping on Fairway up on 102nd Street because they're open pretty late. I can park up there, and they have a really good variety of food. I like to go to the grocer who is right on 93rd and Columbus. I've been going there since Nayo was born, when they first opened up. I buy vegetables and fruits because their produce is really, really good. I like to support the Mom and Pop shops, so that's why I go to that one.

It's good that you like to support them because a lot of supermarkets and other small stores are getting torn down to make new buildings and things like that.
Yes they are. Do you remember the Black bookshop that was on the corner – I think it was Black Books Plus? It was right on Amsterdam. And the sister that owned it actually worked at the Schomburg in Harlem. I loved going to that bookshop. There used to be about four or five bookshops on Columbus. And then once Barnes and Nobles came, they were gone. It was horrific. I was devastated. That's where I used to hang out. You could sit down to read or have conversations. It was really nice when the authors came to sign their books. It was a very informal atmosphere because they were so small. That smallness is really what made it attractive and homey, and that's what I miss. Those big stores just take all that away. When you go to Barnes and Nobles to hear a reader, you have to compete with hundreds of people just to get into the store. It's like the difference between sitting in your grandmother's kitchen on Sunday morning and going to a diner where you don't know anybody.

Yeah, I remember the Black book store. I remember the lady, too. She was very tall, and had glasses. I also remember James Earl Jones. He was signing one of his books, and I remember crawling on him and my mom had to take me off him. That was kind of funny. Now it's a restaurant, and it's very sad. No bookstores. I feel like the neighborhood has lost a lot of its culture. It's just really sad because there are not a

lot of neighborhoods where the culture's really rich and full.

Very nice observation. It really is true. That's why I go to Harlem. Although Harlem is being regentrified. There are a lot of new shops owned by very young brothers and sisters, and I like to go support them. There is one spot that I haven't taken you to yet. It's called the Harlem Tea Room. I live in that place, right on 118th and Madison. When I was a kid, I would have never gone to 118th and Madison because of the gangs. Now, with the regentrification, it's changed so much. It's nice to still see people of color having a participatory part in a neighborhood that was once so full.

I also like going to Harlem.

The Harlem Tea Room has different kinds of teas. They're a little slow with serving the food, so don't ever go in there hungry. But it's a nice atmosphere, very homey. I go in there to work on my papers, have meetings, or if I want to chill out. If I had a hard day working with the kids, I go there and just have a cup of tea and relax. I love talking to Patrice; she's very cool.

After teaching, do you think you're going to do anything else? Do you have any dreams that you still want to fulfill?

Yes. I'm contemplating getting into policy changes. Being an educator, I get very frustrated with things that are set in place by people who are not working with students, children, or parents. It's very frustrating because the system is set up not to function properly. I have a friend who has been teaching since 1968, and she says nothing has changed. That's pretty bad.

I might want to do policy changing work or really work with parents. You're not born with the knowledge of how to parent; it's a learned quality. A lot of parents don't know what they're doing because they didn't come from a family that gave them that structure. The kids ultimately suffer the consequences of that. It's very scary dealing with students, and seeing an eighth grader who is 16 and cannot read. He has made it to the eighth grade, and nobody has been able to catch that. Even the general education students are very volatile. Their anger goes from one to 10, in seconds. That's frightening. Eventually, these young people are going to be adults. If they don't get a handle on how to deal with their anger, it's pretty scary to think where they're going to be in five or six years, not even ten years.

My generation was much more vocal. Your generation seems to be a little more laid back. You don't see as much activism happening; you don't hear people getting angry and making noise about things that go wrong. They just accept it. That's difficult for me to comprehend. How can you accept being treated horribly or being in the situation that you don't have to be in? It comes from knowing that you don't have to be in that situation. You understand what I'm saying?

Yeah. What policies would you change?
Well, I would definitely change education. The schools are still segregated. I don't care what anybody says. The segregation is very visible – even in a city like New York. In the South Bronx, the schools are all Black and Puerto Rican. When you have communities that are not really integrated like that, it's reflected in the classroom.

It's as simple as supplies. I have to struggle to get loose-leaf and pencils. That's obscene. If I want to order books for my students, and I put the order in, it has to go through red tape. I ordered books in August, and I'm still waiting for the books in March. I have to always go in my pocket. I don't have a problem with that, but being a single parent, it creates a problem for me sometimes. You know how I am about reading.

You have teachers who are not going to go that extra mile.

You have teachers who don't really understand how to teach. You have to accept the whole child. Some teachers don't look at it like that: they are there to teach this child how to do A, B, and C. Well, if that child comes in with an attitude, or is hungry, you have to address that. That's going to affect their participation in class. That's going to affect what they learn and what they don't learn. I feel you have to address it.

I would incorporate some type of program for parents. Every parent wants his or her child to do better. I don't care how poor they are, I don't care if they don't work, and I don't care if they do work. Everybody wants the same thing: a better life for his or her child. But people get caught up and categorize people based on the color of their skin, on the amount of education they have, on how they dress, on how they look – it's crazy. This is 2008. Wake up.

Patterns of segregation have changed. With regentrification, neighborhoods that were predominately Black or Hispanic have a lot of Caucasians moving in. Schools are starting to represent that. Some of the schools now have white children in the classroom, and they didn't before. There are not that many because parents go to that school, they look at it, and they ask, "Is this going to benefit my child? Is my child going to be safe? Are there going to be resources for my child?" The parents with money still send their children to private schools or find the better public schools. There are really good public schools. A lot of parents are lazy, so they put their child in the school that's close to where they live because it's more convenient for them. Parents need to really look at the school and ask, "Where is my child going to be all day? What's happening there? How is the principal? How are the teachers? Are they looking out for my child?" I have a lot of issues with the Board of Education even though I'm a teacher.

I love what I do. I love working with kids, I love my daughter, I love hanging out with you. It's exhausting, understanding the different age levels and what's happening developmentally. Constantly having to keep that in mind, keep my mouth shut and understand that it makes no sense trying to have an argument with a teenager because it's a no-win situation. Learning that, understanding that, and being able to apply that.

Bedford-Stuyvesant, Brooklyn
ALYSSA LA CAILLE

THE BEST PLACE ON EARTH

Some of my family and I live in Bed-Stuy, Brooklyn, the best place on earth. I lived in Brooklyn my whole life: 15 years. My mother lived in Brooklyn for 26 years, half of her life. My mother moved to Brooklyn in 1982, 10 years before I was born. She moved because she wanted to relocate with some of her family members. When she arrived in Brooklyn, she knew no one. Trust and believe – as the years went by, she knew everybody and their momma. She's like a little celebrity to the 'hood.

She left Trinidad after 12 years of marriage to my father, Steve, who stayed to handle his business in the army. She came to start a better life and experience new things and different places. When she first touched down to the U.S. she was very excited. She chose Brooklyn because of what she heard from other people. She just so happened to fall in love with Brooklyn. (Who wouldn't?) Before she lived where we live now, in Bed-Stuy on Throop and Hart, she lived on Eastern Parkway where all the West Indian parades and popular shopping areas are. When my mother moved from Trinidad she brought Verleen, my oldest sister; Sherlund, the second oldest; Stevie, the third oldest; and Shanna, the fourth oldest and the last child 'til she came to Brooklyn and had me. Her husband came and met her five years later.

As the years went by and my mother got used to the neighborhood, everybody came to her for help, food, and advice. My mother always worked and took care of her kids. She raised them all by herself while her husband did what he pleased. My mother states she is very proud of her six kids, 17 grandkids, and one great-grandson, Juan Serna Jr.. She loves them all dearly.

JUST A FEW RULES

When people hear about Bed-Stuy's past, they wonder how I survived and how I still live there without wanting to move. It was to the point where a police mobile unit would be on the corner, helicopters overhead, and police cars and vans driving around. There used to be tons of shootings, and when I say tons, I mean tons. Drug dealers would be on the corners with little chicken heads chasing them. Girls would get raped in the Tompkins Projects, three blocks down from my building, or girls would end up missing on Fulton Street. Things like that. There used to be this deli store on the end of my block on Willoughby and Throop where everybody and their mama went to get drugs or whatever they needed.

A warning about Bed-Stuy: trust that in the summer, it can get nasty. People go crazy. In my 'hood they have this saying: "When it gets hot, Black people don't know how to act." That saying is the truth. Shooting, fighting, riots, and everything happen when it gets hot.

There are some good things about my neighborhood, like the new houses they built. The stores and shopping areas aren't that far. If you asked me for a word of advice because you wanted to move there, I would say go for it because you might like it.

There are just a few rules about moving to Bed-Stuy:

#1) Whatever you see, keep it to yourself. Meaning, if you was to see somebody get shot, or see somebody selling drugs, or doing something illegal, keep it to yourself.

#2) Don't snitch. When they say don't snitch, they mean don't snitch. Don't tell on nobody when the cops come to you and ask questions. Whatever you know, keep it to yourself.

#3) Don't think they're your friends 'cause they not. These people who smile and grin in your face are not your friends. When it comes down to beef, they run and start some "he say/she say" bull, and get you into mad stuff.

#4) Whatever you do (selling drugs, etc.), don't let anybody find out. When people find out you are doing things, and they want something and you won't give it to them, and you aren't cool with them or they don't like you, they will snitch. So for your own good, don't let anybody find out.

#5) Last but not least, try earning your respect from day one. I mean, from the day you step foot into Bed-Stuy, make sure people know your name rings bells. Let them know you worship the ground you walk on, and nobody can ever be in control of you but yourself.

THE WHOLE FIVE YEARS OF ELEMENTARY

I went to elementary school in Bed-Stuy, right around the corner from my house. Public School 304 was my elementary school from kindergarten to fifth grade. I went to school every day in uniform, on time, so they were the best school years for me – the whole five years of elementary. When I was in 304, I was more on the boys' side; I never really acted like a girl or dressed like one. I always wore jeans, no shorts or skirts because I always wanted to be covered up. When I think back on how I was then compared to how I am now, I think that was one of the most embarrassing things ever. If it were you, you would be embarrassed too. Now that I'm older, my family brings up those times. It makes me feel so little and weird, like, ill, I was a girl dressing like that.

HOW I MOVE

Middle School 57 was my junior high school on Stuyvesant and Lafayette. Now those were the best days of my life. When I started 57, I was 11 years old, in the sixth grade, and so shy. I didn't speak to anybody. I always did work, came to school on time, and wore the ugly uniform that nobody would ever want to wear. They treated me like a baby because I was the smallest and quietest in my class.

When I got to the seventh grade, everybody knew me, especially the boys and the eighth graders. Every boy in the seventh and eighth grade wanted to go with me, but in seventh grade there was this one boy that I had the biggest crush on. He was the cutest, tallest thing I could ever want to have. I crushed on this boy for the longest. He had a girlfriend, so it messed it up for me, but not for long.

When I got to the eighth grade, everybody knew me and how I moved. The way I moved was simple: respect me, I respect you. Don't look at me, I won't look at you. And if you got a problem, come to me; don't say it behind my back. Eventually, the boy I was crushing on started going out with me. From the beginning of eighth grade until the end and a little longer, everybody in the school knew me and him was going out, so hopefully, they kept their distance. Anyways, at the end of the year I won Prom Queen and he won Prom King, so it was all good. This is exactly why I loved junior high. I will never forget those days.

PAUL ROBESON

I can't say much about this school, except that I wanted out as soon as I walked in. This school was like a jail that hardcore criminals wouldn't want to be in. It was that terrible. The first day I started, I knew I had to get a transfer and get it quick, before it was too late. When I first walked into Paul Robeson, there was this huge fight going on with the upper-class students. Then this boy got caught coming through the scanner with weed on him. Another reason I knew had to leave Paul Robeson was because they searched me, and when they searched me I had to take all my jewelry off, belts and all, so I knew I had to go.

INTERVIEW OF ALYSSA

This is Alyssa, and unfortunately, I'm getting interviewed by my niece, Jeanece.

What was the happiest moment of your life and the saddest?
I have a lot of happy moments, but one of them was my birthday party. It was just a ball, and I had a lot of fun. It wasn't like the rest of my parties. There was something different about it.

The saddest moment. You can name two if you want because I can see your head. . .
You know me too well. The saddest moment was when Christopher and my brother got shot and when I got into the car accident.

Who is the most important person in your life?
My boyfriend Christopher; my mother, of course; my sister; and my nieces and nephews, Jaquan, Jeanece, Laura. I'm not gonna go down the line cause there's about 20 of them.

Who has the biggest influence on your life?
Nobody because nobody can tell me what to do. I do want I want.

If I had to pick – then my niece, Laura, and my older sister, Verleen. Laura has an influence on me, and I look up to my older sister. My mother, sometimes. My sister does the wrong things in relationships, but she doesn't tell me to do the wrong things. She tells me, don't do what she did. I do what I want. It's not like she's putting a gun to my head and telling me what to do. No. She tells me the right things.

When in your life did you feel most alone?
After June 16 all the way until August 13. There was a shooting. I didn't see that person until my birthday, which is August 13.

How has your life been different than what you imagined?
It's different because I pictured myself to be the spoiled brat of the house. Unfortunately, there are four little gremlins under me. I am counting your three younger sisters and your little brother.

Since I was young, my family let me get away with mad stuff. While they disciplined the rest of them, they let me do what I want. That's why, when they try to discipline me now, it's not going to work. They let me do it for too long. Before I got to high school, they were on my case about school. The older I get, the less I care about it, and nobody can change that. In elementary and junior high they were on my case, so it was straight up schoolwork. Back then I was not into boys. I was in my tomboy stage, so I just had my little crushes.

Do you look up to me? Do you want to be like me?

You are one of the people, other than my grandmother, that I call my idol. I look up to you because you're a great aunt. You let me get away with some things that I love. I just love you, and I want to be like you when I get older. You're such a great person to me.

What do you think about your neighborhood?
I love my neighborhood. I have a lot of memories. There's basically one reason why I love Brooklyn, Bed-Stuy: Christopher. Even though I hate it, I just love the fact that he used to be around chasing other people because, either way, I still got to see him.

What are some things that you hate or despise about where you live?

The changes, because it's not going to be Brooklyn no more. The shootings, the abandoned buildings, the cops, the holes, it's just not going to be Brooklyn anymore.

Are there things that happened to you in your past that you regret?

My brother, friend, and Christopher getting shot. And the car accident. I just don't want anything bad to happen, point blank.

Are you afraid of death?

Nobody's supposed to be afraid of death. Nobody can run from death, so you got to take it. Everybody got to go someday. I don't do drugs. I drink wine coolers if I feel overwhelmed or stressed. I don't call it being an alcoholic; I call it having a good time.

Let's bring it back to the questions about your neighborhood. Some things about drugs. Would you ever change some of the things that happened in your family?

If they want to use crack, that's them. I don't think there's nothing wrong with using drugs; just don't come at me sideways with it. That's they life. That's what they want, hey. I still want my gangbanging, little drug dealers, little shootouts here and there, but just no deaths. Okay, just shoot for the fun of it. Shoot in the air, do something, just don't kill nobody. If I don't hate you then I don't wish death, but if I don't like you, so be it. It's nothing you can do – if a person is grown and they want to use it (drugs) there's nothing you can do. I can't change anybody, and nobody can change me. And trust me, there's plenty more things out there that can kill you besides drugs.

IT TAKES TWO

This might sound weird or crazy, but I'm special. I consider myself to have two fathers. Both of their names are Steve, but one is a Jr. and the other is a Sr. I have two fathers because when I was younger my second-oldest brother spoiled me to death. He gave me anything and everything that I wanted. He also did everything for me; he even took me to school with him, and they thought I was his daughter. That's how it is up to this day.

My brother has three kids of his own, two step kids, and a wife. With me by his side, he has six kids in total and a wife. We make one happy family. He was also in the military for a couple of years. That's one thing he and my father have in common. He is helpful to everybody. But he does have his ways when he wants what I cannot deal with. Like, he wants me to go to college, and he always preaches to me about life and what to do and what not to do. At times it does get annoying. It's okay because I always win at the end.

My biological father is way different from my brother. My father expects me to be a genius. He wants college degrees and all. He doesn't believe high school diplomas can get

you far. He does not give me everything I want unless I beg him, and he gets aggravated when I eventually get it. My father has a total of seven kids that I know about: my mother's six and his daughter from some other lady.

My father is from "back in the days," so you know how that goes. He doesn't want me to do anything. He wants me to be how he was when he was growing up, and I don't think that's going to work. How he was disciplined was horrible. My mother wouldn't allow it to happen to me. My father and I hardly ever get along. We live in the same house, and I still don't like talking to him. We don't get along because he wants everything to go his way, and it can't because it has to go my way. I'm the youngest out of all, so I think I should get all the attention. He doesn't give it to me, so I don't talk with him that much.

So now you know my two dads, their similarities and differences, and how I get along and don't get along with them. They both expect different things of me, except they both expect me to finish high school. They hope I go to college.

VERLEEN

You might have heard me talk about my other siblings who are all older than me, but there is one in particular that I care about and love the most. She is the oldest out

of all my mother's kids. She has seven kids and one grandchild. She also has a mother who truly cares about her because she took all seven of her kids and raised them the best way she could. She had a rough childhood growing up. What is so crazy is that she was so pretty (I still consider her to be pretty) until she started using drugs and hanging with the wrong crowd. In my eyes, my sister cannot do anything that I think is wrong. She can do no harm, and I will always love her for the way she is.

She still gives me and everybody else, including her kids, the respect and privacy that they deserve growing up. I still respect her because she is a grown lady and is entitled to do whatever she pleases. Besides everything she does, she still is a daughter, mother, and sister. She gives great advice, and she is very helpful. If she would just leave the drugs alone, things would be so much better.

SUMMER

I like my neighborhood better when the summer first starts than when it comes to the end. I say that because on October 3 there was a shooting right around the corner from my building. Then there was a drive-by across the street by the corner store with a cab that almost hit a lady. It seems like all the drama (the fighting, shooting, drive-bys, etc.) comes at the end of the summer. In my neighborhood, the end of the summer is full of drama and hate, so there is no need for me to get involved in people's business. I go about my business, stay to myself, and do what I have to do.

I like the beginning of the summer because of all the barbeques. The smell of sweet corn and grilled barbeque chicken fills the air. Who wouldn't like that? In July and August, the birthday parties come. We party it up with loud music blasting, people dancing, throwing cake around, kids screaming, and everyone enjoying it. Then comes my birthday party! At one moment I hate when it comes because that means school is close, but I take advantage of that and enjoy my birthday party 'til I can't enjoy it any more.

Then in September, Labor Day comes with the West Indian Day parade. I love that day! I dress up to represent my culture. I wear red, white, and black in the form of my

Trinidad flag. Then it's time for me to rest and go shopping for a back-to-school outfit and books. I get my hair done.

INTERVIEW WITH JEANECE MCLEOD

My name is Jeanece. I'm 13. Today is November 6, 2007. I'm at Grand Central Terminal at the StoryCorps Booth with my aunt, Alyssa.

My name is Alyssa. I'm 15. Tell me some things about the neighborhood that you think I would like to hear.

Sometimes it can be good to live there 'cause most of the time it's quiet and peaceful, but then comes the negative parts where there are a lot of shootings and drug dealers. Bed-Stuy, Brooklyn.

When was the last time something bad happened around your neighborhood?

I believe it was last week Friday, when my cousin Callie got shot.

Was it gang-related?

Yes, it was gang-related. They shot him because they didn't like what he was doing. I guess it was over jealousy.

Do you have any close friends around the neighborhood or at hangout spots?

Most of the people I hang out with are my family. That's about it because around my neighborhood, you cannot trust a lot of people.

Did you go to school in Brooklyn, Bed-Stuy?

Yes I did. I went to school right around the corner from my house. Public School 304. And now, growing up, my little sisters go there too. I'm still in middle school, and the school is Ron Brown Academy, Middle School 57.

Do you have any connections to gang members or anything?

Well, you can say I do. J---, you can call him a gangbanger because he claims he's a Blood. He walks around with the flags hanging out of his pockets, all different color beads, and alla that. A month ago, he got pressed by a boy named D---. He just came up to J---, asking him what's going on. D--- was hearing things around him.

How did they solve their problem?

They solved it because J--- told my uncle. My uncle went up to the person and asked him what happened. He said it's about being Blood and being in gangs. I believe after that it was solved.

Did J--- drop being Blood or does he still claim it to this day?

He claimed to my grandmother that he stopped, but everybody knows he's in it because he doesn't listen. I believe he didn't learn his lesson.

Tell me something else about your neighborhood. Tell me a story you that you would tell anyone who don't live in Brooklyn.

Sometimes it could be a good neighborhood to be around. It's kind of fun once you get to know certain people and not the bad, funny people. Some negative things that they would not like are the shootings, the drug dealers, the crack heads, the bums, and some of the bad things that happen.

Did you ever witness a shooting yourself?

Yes, I did. The shooting was over jealousy and it was right around my building. I think it was four people involved in it; I'm not sure. There were two boys, a grown man, and a girl. I believe he shot the two boys over jealousy.

Did you have a relationship to the two boys that got shot? Did you know them?

Yes, I knew them for a very long time. I was kind of mad and upset because I really don't think they did anything to deserve it. It was over a girl. I think he should never shot nobody over no girl because I believe girls come and go, but he could've took the two boys' lives if he really wanted to, and he was very close to doing that.

Where did the two boys get shot?

In my hallway. One of the boys got shot twice in his leg in the lower part, the other one, which was his brother, got shot in the stomach and the chest. According to the detectives, they still didn't find the shooter, so he's still on the run. I think sooner or later, they will find him, and he will do his jail time.

Did Bed-Stuy ever influence you to do anything you wouldn't do – go against something?

One thing you can say that Bed-Stuy influenced me to not do, is deal drugs. I say it influenced me not to do it because sometimes you may get locked up. You can get killed over it, and also it's no good to do anyways.

Is Bed-Stuy a crazy, mad place, like in the movies where you see people being shot and houses getting raided by the cops? Did you ever see that happen?

One day, across the street from my house, the cops ran up in a house because it was a drug spot. They took a couple of people. There are a lot of deli stores that sell things that they're not supposed to. There are a lot of drug spots like houses that people don't know about, but we'll get to know about, because a lot of people look for drugs when they want it.

Okay, let's drop the drug situation and talk about the little boys and little girls around the neighborhood. How are they?

Well, some of the little boys, mostly they gang bang. They're up to no good, and they just don't go to school when they don't feel like it. They don't do nothing for themselves because all they do is hang out in the street, walk around doing nothing, being stupid. They do graffiti; some of them do drugs; and they just act the fool outside. There are a lot of fast girls around where I live. They like to do a lot of things that they shouldn't be doing at the age that they're doing it. Most of them hang out with some of the boys. They get a bad name around the neighborhood, and then that's what they get called by. I used to get into a lot of trouble, but not now. I just try to stay away from trouble; that's why I stay in the house a lot.

What are some of the things you do to keep from getting into trouble and following the wrong crowd?

I stay inside my house. I stay away from people around my neighborhood. The people I know are no good and will get me into a lot of trouble. That's why most of the times I stay around my family, which is my aunt and my grandmother.

Do you have any other family members besides your aunt and grandmother that live in Bed-Stuy?

Most of my family lives in the dangerous parts, but then, some live in the quiet parts. There are shootings, drive-bys, and all other dangerous things that could happen and make people get killed for no reason.

What are some of the parts you would call dangerous – like certain areas, certain nicknames for the areas?

Flatbush, because there's a whole bunch of gangbanging over there. It's Crips versus Bloods where I live, in Bed-Stuy, Brooklyn. That's where mostly all the Bloods be, and Canarsie – a lot of killings over there. My uncle lives in Flatbush, and some of my friends live in Canarsie.

Where do you go in Bed-Stuy; where are some of your local hangouts spots? Where do you go to have fun with your little friends, if you have any?

Well, around my neighborhood, I don't have a lot of friends because they're no good, and they're troublemakers. Most of the time I just hang out with my sister, who lives downstairs from me. Or, I just stay in my house listening to music or being on the computer.

I bet this is your favorite part. Where do you go to eat?

A lot of places. I like to go to Golden Krust, my favorite. McDonald's. I don't like Burger King like that. KFC, Popeye's. Sometimes when my sister wants to go out, she goes to the Village and goes to Superburgers.

If you had a chance to move, would you?

I don't think I would because I grew up there my whole life, and I like it a lot.

If you had no choice: you just had to move because whoever you lived with wanted to move, where would you move?

I think I'd want to move to somewhere close to where I used to live because I don't want to move. I'd miss it, all the good and bad things that happen. I would miss my friends, my school, and the things I normally do.

What's the best time to be around Bed-Stuy?

Summer, because I like it, but sometimes it's not good to be around Bed-Stuy in the summer, because that's when a lot of fights happen, and shootings. You hear a lot of cops, sirens, all of that.

When the summertime comes, do people really get crazy like they always say?

Yes, they do get crazy because a lot of girls and boys go around just picking fights with each other. Sometimes, if somebody loses playing basketball, maybe because of the heat and the aggravation that they have, they just start fights and shootings.

[StoryCorps Interviewer] When was the craziest summer or the craziest story that you remember happening in the summertime in Bed-Stuy?

A couple of summers ago, I was swinging in the park. There was this basketball game going on, but then it got very serious because one of the teams lost against the other team. Then, all you heard was gunshots, a lot of them. I didn't realize what it was, and I was just sitting there swinging.

[StoryCorps Interviewer] Can you all tell me some stories about Bed-Stuy? Is there anything that's happened that you were both present for that you both remember?

We was just outside one day and there was a shooting going on, and then there was a whole bunch of police. The shooter threw the gun by the building. Helicopters flying. It was a whole big scene. I don't know if it was a Friday or a Saturday night, but we were outside just playing around, acting silly like we usually do, and having fun. It was a drug-dealer issue. Then, there was just like a whole big shooting, just out of nowhere. It was just peace and quiet before it happened, and then all you hear was *pop, pop, pop*. I ran in the building.

I remember that day. We were sitting in front. I was upstairs first, and then something told me to go outside to be nosey because I saw a lot of people crowding around a corner store. Every time people crowd around that corner store, something's happening in it or something's going to happen. So I went outside and that's when I heard the gunshots. I'm trying to run into the building, and while I'm running, Jeanece passes me, and runs up the stairs. When I got in my house I was just sitting there breathing mad hard 'cause people were shooting off the roof of my building, actually.

They were actually trying to go towards my brother and his girlfriend because my brother had gotten into this little incident in the store with this young boy. My brother went home and left it alone. The boy came back with mad people and mad guns. So my brother and his girlfriend faded. I just heard gunshots, but they were mostly trying to get at my brother and his girlfriend driving away in the car.

They were in front of the store, from the projects down the block from my house, Roosevelt Projects on DeKalb, Pulaski, and Marcus Garvey. They were just mad at him and wanted him 'cause of that one little thing he said in the store.

The boy was supposed to be working, and he wasn't. So my brother was like, "Ain't you supposed to be working? You in here for no reason." But everybody around my way knows that's how my brother plays. He always says smart things to people. They saw he was big and wanted to take it out of proportion. The boy wanted to try to be grown about it and try to do something, try to show something like somebody's supposed to be scared that he's gangster. Get outta here.

[StoryCorps Interviewer] So how many guys did he call? So how much time had lapsed?

There were about 30 guys in one corner. My brother had said it around four o'clock. When it started getting late like seven, when people get off the street, that's when we all saw them on the corner. They were sitting outside pointing at my window. That's why I went downstairs. My uncle got mad, too, because they told him that they were going to raid my grandmother's house. That's when it got more out of proportion, and that's why everybody was shooting. Just crazy.

[StoryCorps Interviewer] Where did your brother end up going?

My brother left. He went home to Flatbush. We called him and said, "This boy talking about he's gonna raid the crib, shoot up our house." He came back to squash it. My brother called the cops and said that the guy was threatening his mother and alla this. The cops said, "Well, we don't find a gun on him, so we can't do anything. If he says something else, then that's for you to do whatever you got to do." As soon as the cops left, that's when those same boys came back and just tried to start shooting.

We call that corner Death Row because everything happens on that corner. There's a stop sign but no lights, so cars keep crashing, accidents keep happening.

Shootings happen on that one corner, drive-bys, everything. That's a little death row right there.

I think that the craziness rubbed off on a lot of your siblings and little nephews and nieces because a lot of them don't handle it like me. I sometimes tend to act crazy and act like I don't have it all, too. That's why I love this. I could never move out of it. I don't want to leave because the best memories. They could change everything they want: bus stops, stores, I don't care. I still won't ever move as long as they keep my building the same.

[StoryCorps Interviewer] So where do you all see yourselves in 20 years? Do you see yourselves like your older sisters or your mother?

In 20 years, I don't know. I think I be a little bit like my older sister 'cause everybody already says that I act like her. I kind of look like her. Certain things she did when she was younger, they say I do it now

In 20 years, I'll be 33. I think I would be finished with college, hopefully, and be what I want to become, which is either a lawyer or a teacher.

That's the same two things I wanted to be, but I don't want to be a lawyer any more because they lie to people to protect people who don't deserve to get protected. So I want to be either a prosecutor or a cop. I'm tired of lawyers and their lies. The reason I decided to be a cop or a prosecutor is because of what the shooter did to those two boys in my hallway. His mother just ran to get him a lawyer, and I didn't think that was right because he had no business doing that. That's why I don't want to be a lawyer any more, because I'd be defending people like him, knowing they did wrong. I don't care how much money you pay me, I can't do it. I don't know how they sleep at night. I'm not defending you if you did something wrong. I'd rather prosecute you and put you where you belong.

[StoryCorps Interviewer] Do you all have any closing remarks?

That Bed-Stuy is great. Bed-Stuy is the best. My mother's trying to move down south. She loves Bed-Stuy but she wants to go down south, and I do not want to move. I believe down south is too quiet. They say it's a lot like Tennessee. That's why I refuse to move. I love Bed-Stuy to death.

Bedford-Stuyvesant, Brooklyn
MAKEDA GAILLARD-BENNETT

QUEEN OF SHEBA

I blessed this world on August 31, 1991, at Long Island College Hospital. I was named Makeda after the Queen of Sheba. I reside in the Rotten Apple, also known as New York City, home of the crooked cops, gangs, gunshots, crack heads, dope fiends, and your occasional bums in the subway. Besides that, I love it here. It's not all bad; there's beauty to be found. This is where I had my first fights, heartbreaks, and memories.

I live in the Bed-Stuy section of Brooklyn with my mother and my younger brother. Outside of Jamaica, it's the only place I know. My grandmother emigrated to the States and eventually to Brooklyn in the early '60s, where she had my mother.

My mother is a strong-willed woman and a single parent. We've lived in a few places in Brooklyn over the years. My mother made sure that each place we moved to was either bigger in space or on a better block. My mother avoided the projects because she didn't want us surrounded by explicit activity that could corrupt our minds.

The drama, tears, trials, and tribulations I experienced formed and sculpted the girl I am today.

BED-STUY: DO OR DIE

Staring at the century-old brownstones built with marble fireplaces, mahogany staircases, double-sliding doors, window shutters, and stone-carved facades, you'll find it hard to believe these homes are in Bedford-Stuyvesant, Brooklyn. There's little left of the cracked asphalt, abandoned lots, and boarded-up buildings that have kept people away.

Back in the day, Bed-Stuy took up the slogan "Do or Die," which meant you were either with the program or not. At the time, it was one of the toughest places to live in Brooklyn and feared by the surrounding neighborhoods. It was called the largest Black neighborhood in the U.S. Over the years, it has been a cultural center for Brooklyn's African-American population. This started in the 1930s when Blacks left an overcrowded Harlem upon the opening of a new subway line, to find more housing availability in Brooklyn.

In my neighborhood, I pass by restored houses that were used as stops on the Underground Railroad. My last house on Chauncey Street was renovated but still had some things that hadn't been used since the late 1800s, like the dumbwaiters in my kitchen. Retailers are now asking for a pretty penny for the brownstones in my neighborhood, which used to go for much less. A lot of places that were significant in my neighborhood have been knocked down to make room for new developments. They don't have the same essence of community. When the old folks of the block sit around and watch the many changes and construction, they usually mutter, "Yep, they moving in all right." It was predominantly a Black neighborhood, but now there are white or Asian families moving in.

The historic neighborhood is rich in culture and excitement. In the summers in the park, there are jazz and R&B concerts and Friday Night Movies in August. The vibes and rhythm that are always bumpin' make my neighborhood feel like home. I know what you are thinking: it seems too divine to be in Brooklyn. There are also fights, boys trying to bag some girl's number, cursing, yelling, smoking, drinking, and drug-use.

But even in the "nicer" places like the suburbs, there are secrets and a few skeletons in those walk-in closets. No matter where you go, there's always going to be a smudge on a beautiful picture. Just think of it that way.

HALSEY STREET

I've lived in Bed-Stuy for the majority of my life but moved around three times in the neighborhood. First I lived on Halsey Street, which was a fairly okay block. It was far from my favorite because there were always men on the corners either calling out to my female cousins and me or just being loud and unruly. Besides the noise and such, I had the most fun there. All my friends lived over there, and I knew just about everyone. My aunt's house was where everyone on the block came together and helped one another out. I loved living over there back in the days, but now I've grown up and am looking for a different scene.

CHAUNCEY STREET

Then, I moved to Chauncey Street. Though it was only a few blocks from Halsey Street, there I lived on a quiet block with a mixture of people. My neighbors were Black, white, and Asian. Although it was a nice and well-kept block, everyone was Rosy-the-Nosey-Neighbor. Everyone knew everyone's business. Some people did keep to themselves and looked down on other people and often shook their heads in disapproval at the teenagers when we got loud. I lived right across the street from Fulton Park. On holidays, especially New Year's Day, there was always shooting. From Chauncey you could barely hear it; it seemed like a sound fading in the distance somewhere, though the projects were two blocks away.

DECATUR STREET

I then moved to Decatur Street, where I am currently living. It is around the corner from the projects. We were there for New Year's Eve, 2007. "3, 2, 1 – Happy New Year!" we yelled in unison. My mother popped the bottle and poured the apple cider, while my brother stuffed his mouth full of grapes. I proceeded to the dining room and signed onto the computer to send MySpace comments entitled, "Happy New Year! Hope you had fun!"

Pow! Pow! The gunshots were loud in our ears, because they had been fired in the parking lot of the mini-projects behind my house. A car alarm went off. My brother and I were not so surprised, yet I jumped a little bit in shock. We made it our duty to fake scream and yell – "They shooting! They shooting!" – reenacting a scene from a comedy TV show. Running and ducking behind our coffee table in the living room, we laughed at our silliness. I turned our attention to the celebrities on TV and envied their extravagant lifestyle. I heard my mother in the background speaking to a police officer, complaining about the shootings that were still occurring, afraid that a stray bullet would strike someone.

Bang! Bang! The shots still ringing in my ears, I cautiously got up and closed the windows. I still heard it, only this time it sounded more like a faint whisper.

Despite the fact that there are shootings, my landlord and neighbors are friendly if you're friendly. We live across the street from a playground, where there are fights between little kids and teenagers. I don't mind it because by now I'm used to it. Just a few blocks up where my friend lives are the Weeksville Projects and I like chillin' over there on the weekend or after school. I feel welcomed since I've known all this all my life, pretty much.

MY OLD LOOK

When I first moved to Bed-Stuy, I was maybe eight. My aunt and family already lived out there, so it wasn't like I didn't know anybody, but they didn't live on my new block. I was the new girl on the block with a little brother who had to go with me everywhere I went. I was afraid that even if I tried to make friends, he would be there to somehow mess it up. Surprisingly he didn't – well, not all the way; he was sociable when he was younger.

At the time, I was skinny and had dreadlocks, which I wore long, wild, and out, or in a ponytail. With a baby's face, I usually got mistaken for a boy. I remember one time, my mother and I were walking on Fulton Street. I'm not exactly sure why; all I remember was that I was highly upset because my mother forced me to wear this blue, hideous corduroy dress, which I hated. We were just coming out of a bodega, and a lady my mother knew stopped us. After speaking to her, she "complimented" me by saying, "My, what a handsome son you have." I thought that was incredibly unbelievable since I was wearing that dress, and I figured that was the first thing you saw when you looked at me.

It seemed like no matter what I did, I didn't feel welcomed in my neighborhood. Now I can care less, but for a child, that's the worse feeling ever. My mother didn't like the schools in Bed-Stuy so I went to schools further out: East Manhattan School, David Grayson Christian Academy, Public School 282, and Satellite 3 Academy, Williamsburg Prep High School, and now, Urban Academy.

P.S. 282, which was in Park Slope, was a good school. I knew everyone there and had my clique of friends. I did my work but got in trouble a lot. I stayed occupied in my after-school program at Congregation Beth Elohim, where I took hockey, soccer, crochet, and lanyard classes. I took ballet and modern dance in Jamaica, Queens and all types of art classes at Pratt Institute.

I only wore what I thought was comfortable: jeans, sneakers, and old t-shirts. I didn't give much thought about my appearance. I was only a kid living a carefree life. While the girls my age played hopscotch, Double Dutch, and exchanged their Christmas Barbie dolls, I played basketball, rode my bike, played Hide and Go Seek, Red Light / Green Light, and Steal the Bacon. I didn't care about any Barbie dolls or the latest gossip. My mother knew not to buy me Barbie Dolls or any type of baby dolls. I envied the fact that boys got the BMX racecars and such.

MY NEW LOOK

I thought Shawn, who also lived on the block, was really cute. He was probably 12. We played a lot of basketball together. He had brown skin, short curly hair, and a baby face. I'm not exactly sure what attracted me to him; maybe it was because he considered me to be one of his "homies." Or, maybe it was the fact that he sucked his thumb, and his top teeth curved. When he smiled, he made all the girls melt. I didn't want to be just a friend, but that was all he saw me as.

I thought I could be just more than just friends with Shawn, but the day I realized I couldn't, I figured there had to be time for a change. I vividly remember it like it was last week. I woke up that Saturday morning. After throwing on my mom's old Essence Jazz Fest T-shirt, faded jeans, and old Nike sneakers, I grabbed my skates and basketball. I knew I would be playing a game of street basketball with the boys: Sammy, David, Jay, Brian, Brendan, and, of course, Shawn. I met up with them and we started our game. We played against some kids from around the corner, and we won. Sitting on the front stoop down the block, licking ices from the ice man, we contemplated whether we should play again or go to someone's house to play video games. Up the block came Stephanie, Shaniqua, and her sidekick, Lisa.

"Hey Shawn, what ya'll doin'?" asked Shaniqua, smiling bright, showing off the cherry-red lip-gloss that was heavily coated on her little lips.

"Nothing much, you?" replied Shawn, staring at her.

"If ya'll not doing nothing, why don't ya'll come with us to Lisa's house. . . to chill?" Stephanie said, as the girls giggled in union.

"A'ight, come on," Shawn said, and we started walking up the block.

I secretly knew that trouble was waiting ahead; that's what those girls were good for. I didn't want to go, so I tried to tell the Crew in hints not to go along.

"So we not going to finish playing our game?" I asked to no one in particular, hoping Shawn would speak up.

Before Sammy was about to agree with me, Stephanie butted in saying, "Makeda, you don't have to go. We really wanted the guys to come along." Laughing, and giving her girls a high-five, she added, "Don't no one want you to come. Look at you – you dress like a boy. C'mon step your game up."

I was about to charge at her when Shawn came between us and said, "Chill Makeda, she just joking. You don't *have* to come."

I stared hard at him with watery eyes trying to decode what he had just said. *You. Don't. Have. To. Come.* I individually assessed Sammy, David, Jay, Brian, and Brendan, who were now all hovering over Lisa, Shaniqua, and Stephanie. At that moment I realized how much I *wasn't* welcomed. Lisa, Shaniqua, and Stephanie were all fully developed in imaginable areas and sported the latest outfits. I, on the other hand, was busy with sports and nothing too much in particular. *I couldn't possibly compete with them.* Hot tears now formed in my eyes, blurring my vision. Blinking rapidly, I knew my tears were on the verge of rolling down onto my sweaty face. But I couldn't and wouldn't give them the satisfaction of seeing me cry. I felt the now-finished ice thick and cold in the pit of my stomach. My stomach was churning, and I tasted my salty sweat in the corners of my mouth. More sweat was pouring down the sides of my face and my forehead. My underarms itched and my arms twitched. I vividly pictured myself knocking the living daylights out of Stephanie and her sidekicks.

Before I knew it, I felt my lips moving but couldn't quite hear what I was saying. It felt like a movie, rolling in slow motion: the camera zooming up close and personal to my messy face, to Shawn and his worried face, then to my so-called friends, and then lastly stopping at the Big-booty Trudy's face. "Fuck you," I spat at Stephanie. I ran back up the block with so much speed I could have sworn there was dust flying behind me like in the cartoons. No wonder later in my life I decided to run track. I ran into my house at full speed and headed straight for my room, past my mother in the kitchen on the phone with my Godmother. I sobbed hard on my bed, still with my dirty sneakers on, curled up in a fetal position, my head throbbing. I tried to squeeze my eyes tight to block out the scene that was playing over and over again in my head.

My 10th birthday was right around the corner, and I knew what I wanted. I wanted to cut off my locks off and get braids and curls and a cute outfit. For the next couple of weeks I didn't go outside, I just woke up and went to the couch to watch TV all day. My mother's close friend, Katrina, came over and braided my hair. It came out really nice and really tight, too. I cried the whole time because it hurt like hell.

When I finally did come outside a day after my birthday, I was walking to the bodega at my corner, and I spotted Shawn on the back of Brendan's bike, on the pegs. I tried to retain a cool demeanor and walked with my head high. Walking back out of the corner store, bopping my head to my new tape player, I saw Shawn, Brendan, Sammy, David, Jay, Brian, Lisa, Shaniqua, and Stephanie sitting on the little stoop in front of my building. I knew what was up; I could just tell that Shawn and Brendan had told them about "my new look."

"Hey, Makeda, nice hair." Sammy said, smiling hard at me.

"Uh, thanks," I replied, trying to get past them into my building. "Excuse me, Lisa," I said through clenched teeth.

"Makeda, don't try it. Don't think you cute." Stephanie said.

At that instant, I spun around and swung my right fist at her. I hit her with the first blow, but Shawn came between us once again, "Makeda, calm down."

All the anger that had built up inside of me was now spilling out. "Shut the fuck up. You stay defending her. Just leave me alone!" I yelled, and pushed past everyone and ran up the five flights to my house. Finally in my home, I rested my head against my metal front door and smiled to myself. Not really knowing why, I had a good feeling.

I realized that I needed to stick to what society laid out for females like me. I usually heard comments like, "Why she always running 'round here with these boys like she don't have any sense? Doesn't she know that isn't how a young lady's supposed to act?" So I traded in my sneakers for a pair of shoes and jeans for skirts.

INTERVIEW WITH MY MOTHER

December 16, 1971 was the date. Born into a Jamaican family at Kings County Hospital in Brooklyn, New York, my mother, Cheryl Bennett, lived the first few years of her life in Jamaica. Upon coming back to America, she lived on St. Johns Place in

Prospect Heights, Brooklyn with her family, which consisted of her mother, stepfather, two younger brothers, and a sister. Later, they moved to Bed-Stuy, Brooklyn, where she lived until she went off to college. Still favoring the neighborhood afterwards, she moved back, renting an apartment with her two children.

She is not only my caretaker but also a friend. She means a great deal to me, and even though I know the majority of her life story, it still excites me every time I hear it. It didn't dawn on me until recently that she struggled as a young adult herself. I also realized that as I get older, she gives me better insight into her life. She no longer holds back or sugarcoats anything, as she did when I was younger.

on growing up

I would really say I grew up in Prospect Heights, Brooklyn, from when I was seven to 18.

What was your childhood like there?
My childhood was fun. I definitely wasn't the rich kid on the block. Yet, I wasn't the poorest kid on the block. At the same time, back then, things were cheaper and you were able to. . .

Get by?
Make do with whatever you had. That's living in the ghetto. Even though there was a park not too far away, no one sent his or her children to the park to play. They just sent them outside to play on the block. There were lots of games. Tag, Freeze Tag, Peas and Butter, and other very simple games that we made out of nothing. Double Dutch, jump rope, hand games. I don't see them being played any more. A lot of kids on the block – that's who your friends were. That's who you cliqued up with. A lot of times you had maybe five to 10 best friends in any given year.

childhood nowadays

You mentioned that you played simple games when you were a child. Do you think that children now are worse or better than in your time?
I just don't see them playing kid games anymore. A lot of the games we played were outside and just came up for us. It was safe for us to just go outside to play. For whatever reason, maybe because I was a child, it just seemed like the days were longer. We didn't have all this after-school remediation help. We just went to school, eight-thirty to three o'clock. If your mother was working or something, you went to an after-school program, like a daycare center, and stayed there until your mother picked you up. You

did your homework there, or maybe they helped you with your homework. You had something to eat and time to play board games or dodge ball. Simple things like that. When we came home, we probably played outside while dinner was being made, and we ate and then sat and watched TV together or something like that. It seemed like the days were much longer.

family

My family is from Jamaica – both Mother and Father. I was raised by my mom, so I had a closer bond to my mother's side of the family. When I speak about my family I'm speaking about my mother's side. In the early- to mid-'60s they had these programs. They might have them now, I don't know. They sponsored students from Jamaica to come to America. A few of my mother's friends were a part of that program, and that's how she came here. She was pretty much the only one here. She had an aunt here, but a lot of times, family is in name only, not so much in truth.

Even though my mother and I didn't really communicate a lot, we communicated much more when she was sick, in the year before she passed. She died when she was 49, on July 11, 1993. In the months leading up to that, we were much more open and able to discuss things on an adult-daughter to mother level. By that time you were already born, so perhaps that also enabled us to talk more. If she were still alive, I would foster a more positive, open relationship with her.

There has been a constant figure throughout my life and that would be my best friend's mom. She's somewhat of a surrogate mom to me.

school

I could read very fast, and I read a book a day. I read everything. A blessing for me was that I went to what was touted as a "gifted and talented" junior high school. It would probably be what they call a specialized junior high school. I attended Satellite West, and at the time, there were three schools like that. It was just about academics. It would probably be the equivalent of Stuyvesant High School or Bronx High School of Science or Brooklyn Tech. It wasn't as stringent, even though they did pay good attention to academics. There were also a lot of arts in the school.

1970s & 1980s

Back then, it was good when you had a dollar. If you had a quarter, you could still get stuff. You could buy candy; you could buy an icey. There were so many things you could still buy for a quarter or 35 cents. Chips were like, 15 cents. You could also buy penny candies or two-for-five cent candies. I mean, there were so many things you could've done at that time. I had that carefree feeling. In the '70s, there were so many different songs. The early days of hip-hop were really like disco. These were people from the 'hood but as it got more. . .

urban?

Don't use "urban." It started in the ghetto. By the time the 80's came in, disco was dead. So the '80s became much more fashion conscious. You had Levi's, Lee Jeans with the permanent crease in it. Adidas, sheepskins, leather jackets, Kangols, Yves Saint Laurent glasses, leather V-Bombers. People got killed for their Yves Saint Laurents. People also got killed for their sheepskins. I guess it still happens. People have gotten killed for their. . .

Now it's Jordans.
People have gotten killed over their iPod, but killed over Jordans?

I remember in eighth grade there was this boy – I forget his last name, but his first name was Jason. He was such a punk, but I guess his parents had money. They lived over there on the border of Park Slope and Prospect Heights in one of those high-rise buildings, so they must have had money. He would come always so fresh with his Le Tigre shirts (because that's what we had then –it wasn't so much the IZOD shirts but also the Le

Tigre shirts) with his Lees or Levis. Pumas in this color and that color – so on and so forth. So we went to Satellite West, which was like up the block from some housing projects where the bad kids hung out. They knew the good, corny kids went to Satellite West, so they would always try to jack us or do something to us. The 37 bus used to run on that block. We would always get on in front of the school because no one would wait in front of the projects. One time, an older guy got on the bus, and he stood next to Jason. He looked down at his sneakers, and he was like, "Yo, what size are those?" He said, "Seven" or whatever it was, and the man was like, "Yo, run them." And so Jason took off his sneakers and gave them to the dude, who just exited the bus. Jason just stood there in his socks, on the bus, waiting until the bus pulled off. And he just shrugged it off, opened up his book bag, and pulled out another pair of sneakers. He just stood there, like, "'What? What?'" You just got your sneakers stolen, and you think you're bad because you pull out another pair?

race & color

As a child did you have any self-hatred because of the whole light skin, dark skin situation?

I didn't. I was neither light skinned nor dark skinned. Not that it didn't affect me. I was too light to be dark but too dark to be light, so I was almost invisible.

Do you think that took a toll on you growing up? Did you ever wish to be one kind or something?

I had couple of friends that I grew up and played with around the way for a long time. If there were six of us, four of them were very ghetto. Gold rings, gold teeth, gold nails, even. Doorknockers, the hairstyles, the whole fad, and everything like that. I guess they were very ghetto fabulous. That's what you would call it today. It just so happened that they were also very light skinned. So those were the ones that always got the guys. Trust me, it wasn't because they were beautiful. It was just the fact that they were light skinned and then on top of that, all the adornment that they would wear.

neighborhood

What do you like most about your neighborhood?

I really wanted to get back to that side of town, but the rental prices were out of my price. By this time, I had already moved to Bed-Stuy because it was more affordable at that time. Now, it's pretty much moved out of our price, but you can still find good people here and there, so you can find somewhere affordable.

We're a middle-class family. No matter how low it got, we did not want to move to the projects. That was not an option. The places we live seem to get better and better. Even though I prefer the last house we lived at, I still like this area. It's on a fairly decent block, despite the shootings and the back window that you keep closed.

I don't believe anybody that moves into the projects necessarily wants to. I think it's probably more of a difficult circumstance that makes someone move into the projects; they just get caught up in a cycle and just happened to be there.

Sometimes, I hate living over here. Not hate it necessarily, but I get tired of it. If you had a house in Bed-Stuy, would you want to stay here or move out?

Anyone who knows me knows I've been trying to leave New York. I would love to have the home with the front yard and the back yard. Unfortunately it's not that easy to do when you're poor. It's just what it is, being here and only being able to afford rent. There were many times I wanted to leave, but different things came up. There wasn't really a support system for me anywhere else. When you lay down roots somewhere, it's kind of hard to uproot and go somewhere else. It's hard if you have children; you can't just pick up and leave because you want the best school system, or the best education, or the best environment. It's hard to do when you move into a new place. You don't know where that good school is. My neighborhood has become comfortable to a degree because this is what I know. I was born and raised here, and I try to maneuver the best way I can here.

CHARLENE HARRIS

My aunt, Charlene Harris, who's only in her early 20s, is like a big sister to me. When I was growing up, I was like her shadow: everywhere she went, I tagged alongside her. I remember a time when I was eight. My aunt had been boiling hot water for a bath. The kitchen was downstairs and she was taking the pot of water to the upstairs bathroom. I didn't know she was coming upstairs slowly while I ran down the steps two at a time. BAM! I ran directly into her, spilling the hot pot of water on both of us. I accidentally rubbed my shirt onto my skin, trying to get the hot water off of me. I suffered from a slight burn on the left side of my stomach.

Water really didn't agree with us. When she was a little girl, age six, and I was only a year old, we both took a bath at the same time. My grandmother stepped out of the room while we played. I flipped myself over and was lying face down in the shallow bath water. I couldn't flip myself back over. My aunt was shocked at the sight of me struggling and became statue-like, wanting to reach out and help me but scared frozen. My grandmother must have sensed a problem from the next room. She returned and, in a rush, helped me out of the water. She scolded my aunt for not acting quickly.

My aunt now acts with more caution with her own son, Nicholas. The tables have turned, and it's three-year-old Nicholas who is like my shadow: he tags along everywhere I go.

I am very similar to my aunt. We have tomboyish ways, attitude, and comical humor. My family would say she can be self-centered, but she also has her good moments. I miss the old days, when I would always be at her house where my grandpa, uncles, and my oldest uncle and his family lived. It was a full house in the three-family home in Bed-Stuy, when more of my cousins came to visit on weekends. She was the cool aunt: living carefree, always having fun. We kids secretly looked up to her.

FOOLISH THOUGHTS

Lounging on the concrete steps, I rest my body on the cool iron railing for back support and cool relief of some sort. I gaze at the flickering street lamps. *On. . . Off. . . On.* My mind wanders, and seems to drift a thousand years away. I try to re-cap and re-live my childhood years. Imagining I was still that young, innocent, carefree, skinny, knock-kneed little girl I used to be, always anxious to run over to my aunt Charlene's house to go play. Bright-eyed and with a huge smile usually glistening with cherry-flavored Ice Pop, I waited for my name to be called when playing a game of Freeze Tag on the ol' block with the neighborhood kids. I hear the voices of loud-talking people and laughter, as if I were there, back in time.

A second later, I'm in the present once again. I'm back on the old concrete stoop, leaning against the hard railing. It's not fun anymore. The stoop where I spent most of my wasted time doesn't feel the same, just cold and empty. There isn't any more Freeze Tag or Hopscotch, just my distant memories and me. We've all grown up now. I stand up to look down the block, as if expecting to see my old friends skipping towards me to see if I'd join them in a game of Steal the Bacon. I squeeze my eyes tight shut, hoping and wishing to re-live the times I most yearn for. The past has escaped me and the future scares me. What will I do? Who will I be? All the questions boggle my mind. A cool breeze hits me, and I'm suddenly more alone than I've ever been. This feeling is too overwhelming. Sighing at my foolish thoughts, I return inside the house, and the front door creaks shut with a *click*.

Peter Cooper Village, Manhattan
Carnasie, Brooklyn
ZAIRA SIMONE

"MOVING ON UP"

On March 1, 2007, my brother, Mohammed Cody, and his wife, Tisha Andrea Peters, moved into a three-bedroom apartment on East 89th and Ave N in Seaview, Canarsie. They were fed up with living in Crown Heights and dealing with shady landlords who couldn't maintain their building and were constantly increasing the rent. They would complain about the leaking ceiling in the bathroom and about the so-called maintenance man, who kept messing with the boiler. During the winter, the floors in their house were so cold and damp, one had to put on extra pairs of socks. The neighborhood also seemed miserable, especially when it snowed, because the garbage men wouldn't collect the garbage for days, and you would find mounds of frozen trash.

Besides being concerned about the condition of the neighborhood, they were also concerned about their children's school. They had to make a decision quickly. Should they continue to allow the landlord to rip them off, or should they find a place that was suitable and affordable? As Tisha states: "We both made the decision; neither of us could stand that place any more. We were desperate for a move, and I was getting ready to have Sapphire. It was stressful."

The rest of the family was happy to hear that my brother found a place. But there were also people who worried about the distance and how Tisha would cope with the baby alone in an empty house while my brother was working in Midtown and the other two kids were at school. I think Tisha and my brother moved to Canarsie to get away from all the nosey relatives, who were only good for talking. My mother was also happy for them, though she got tired of taking the long trips. However, when the weekends came, she would hop right on that bus with her MP3 player and her knitting, waiting to cuddle with my newborn niece and bug the hell out of my brother.

I remember the first time I went to their house. I woke up early to make sure I got a head start on the journey. It was so cold that day; there was sleet and snow everywhere. The skies were clear, the sun was shining, and this was my only chance to go. By the time I arrived in Seaview, I was exhausted. But as soon as I got off the bus, my whole body awoke. The streets were paved with clean snow, and there were brick houses. Everything felt like a Nat King Cole Christmas special, except for the Parang music blaring, "Mama drink a rum and a punchin cream. Dis is Christmas mornin, I say drink if ya drinkin. . . wine if ya whinin. . . but don drink if ya drivin." I just felt so good. Most of all I was glad when I saw my niece and nephew gleaming through the window in their pajamas. Before I even approached the door, they shouted, "Aunty, you see our house?"

LIVING BETWEEN WORLDS

I was born in Bedford-Stuyvesant, Brooklyn and raised partly in South Africa. From the age of one, I owned a passport. I traveled with my father to Ghana, South Africa, Senegal, Mozambique, Lisbon, and Holland. At the age of five, I lived in Johannesburg, South Africa, and attended the Sacred Heart Catholic School. Now, I live in Peter Cooper Village with Karin Santi, who is my stepmother. This is just my residence and, sad to say, nothing more than that. Unlike many people, who love their local coffee shop and know their neighbor, I don't share a connection to Peter Cooper Village. You don't see a lot of diversity here because the place is crawling with middle-class and rich white families.

Diversity at its best in Peter Cooper Village can be seen on the playgrounds, which are occupied by nannies from the English, Spanish, and French Caribbean. There are also nannies who are Indian, Creole, Black, and even Eastern European. Can you picture an old Ecuadorian woman speaking Castilian Spanish to two toddlers, who speak both Spanish and French? It's amazing how cosmopolitan this place has become. However, outside of these playgrounds, this beautiful portrait disappears.

I have a problem with the lack of diversity in the complex. The only people of color I see are the nannies. I remember the time when an old Grenadian woman approached me, asking if I knew any family that needed a housekeeper. The woman had a bundle of notices, which she was planning to hang up all over Peter Cooper Village. I felt a little awkward that she chose to ask me this question. I directed her to the complex, and told her she could just hang those notices on the bulletin boards inside of the building. My perspective on these jobs is that the people work very hard just to provide for their families. A job is a job, yet this field of work is demeaning to a certain extent. No one wants to clean up after someone, but in reality people have bills to pay and mouths to feed.

I wasn't happy to be asked if I know any families who needed house cleaning. I don't think that I'm being too sensitive, because the woman obviously assumed that I didn't live in the neighborhood, but that I probably worked there. Is it the woman's fault for asking? The woman is not to blame, but would you find this woman asking people about house cleaning in Seaview, Canarsie? Probably not.

This experience made me question how I felt about being a Black woman in Peter Cooper Village. The truth is, I don't really pay much attention to whether I am one of the minorities. I think it is insane to even count myself in a category every time I come in and leave the complex. It's like walking around with a sign that reads "I'M BLACK." One doesn't just function in that way and if one does, he or she is dealing with some sort of insecurity. Some call it a mental-slavery thing. You know that attitude that some people have, as if the whole world has dumped all the trash on them, and everyone is responsible for their hardships.

In Seaview, Canarsie, you would not really find yourself in a situation like this, because the majority of people who live there are Black working-class families. It's not to say that the old woman who approached me could not belong to the Peter Cooper community, but the fact that she approached me there says something. She obviously knew that there are some wealthy families who needed a hand to cook and clean after them. In Peter Cooper Village almost everyone has a nanny or a housekeeper. I'm the exception simply because my ethic is to clean after myself, and besides, I didn't grow up with a silver spoon in my mouth. I can't even afford to have someone clean my house; I'm more concerned with getting money for college. The "minorities" in Seaview are doctors, bus drivers, food caterers, and schoolteachers. Seaview is a melting pot, embraced by everyone. You won't find only one Black person, or be told, "Speak English, you're in this country." At the same time, it is not unusual to find women who used to be nannies or housecleaners who now live in Seaview. Their professions have changed and their stories are concealed.

The woman who approached me at Peter Cooper Village is not just a nanny who cares for other people's kids. She has a family of her own. She is not just the housekeeper who cleans up after others. She sweeps her own floors and may have others cook for her. She's a dreamer, a student, a mother, a daughter, and a wife. You may find her as that old woman who bickers about politics or about what a woman is supposed to be. She lectures you on the mistakes you have made and what not to do the next time. These women are strong; they have made many sacrifices for the next generations. Whenever I see one of these women in Seaview, I always wonder, "What is her story?"

FROM ONE SIDE OF BROOKLYN TO ANOTHER

I never liked Canarsie because it is so far from the train. There are no local stores and cinemas. There is no social life that exists in Canarsie. When my brother moved to Seaview in Canarsie and I needed a break from the crazy people in my mother's neighborhood, I would get right on the bus. These rides are about an hour long, but I needed relief from the Pratt Institute yuppies and the Lafayette Garden people. My mother lives on the other side of Brooklyn, which is very different from Seaview. The area where she lives is known as the central part of Brooklyn, which connects Bed-Stuy with Williamsburg.

Pratt yuppies are the new residents who have established cafes, bistros, and boutiques. They are the artsy, youthful class of gentrifiers who attend Pratt Institute. I have seen them buying marijuana from the local drug dealers and playing craps in front of their apartments. Some members of the community, predominately landlords, accept their presence. However, they refuse to assimilate into the neighborhood or communicate with others on a personal level. Even their favorite hangout, "Sputnik," is exclusive and rejects the people who live in the projects. Throughout the past two years, there has only been one Latino working in there. I am not prejudiced against the yuppie community, but I think they don't contribute to the neighborhood in any way, nor am I fan of gentrification.

The Lafayette Garden people are known as the first residents of the neighborhood, and they fight to claim their territory against the yuppies and the police. In the Lafayette Garden projects, you will find young aspiring actors, rappers, warlords, police officers, and hard-working families. When I moved back from London, it saddened me

so much to see kids who I went to elementary school with now drug dealing or having dropped out of high school.

These were the many reasons why I would visit my brother in Canarsie. The neighborhood that I once knew was changing, and I didn't fit. I wasn't related to any of these groups of people, and I preferred for things to be that way.

Seaview is very diverse. Many of the residents in the neighborhood are working-class families. The majority of residents are Italian, Jewish, West Indian, and Asian. The neighborhood is also now integrated, whereas in the early '70s it was not. Between the early '70s and late '90s, it was hard for many Black families to move into the area because it was occupied by many Italian families, who, in some ways, had the power to choose who moved into the neighborhood. During this time, not much real estate in Canarsie was being sold to Blacks and other minorities. However, many Jewish real-estate owners began to rent to Black families, specifically people coming from the Caribbean. Many of these owners believed that they would gain much revenue from renting to new immigrant families, because many were refusing to move into federal housing.

Seaview is green and quiet. The architecture almost seems to replicate that of Colonial times. There are houses painted in yellow and cream, with huge lawns of cedar trees and beautiful flowers. There are Black people who drive SUVs or classic Porsches. Beautiful Grenadian construction men reside there, bickering about the World Cup while renovating their stairs.

THE SOUCOUYANT

In Seaview, I enjoy seeing the hundreds of cars that pull up to this old woman's house. She supposedly cooks the best jerk chicken in Brooklyn. I never tasted her food, but I can always smell it from across the street. At first, I didn't understand why there were so many people visiting this house. Then I heard that she runs a catering business from her home. She makes this good jerk chicken and black cake. During the summer when everyone is out on their stoops, you always see people gazing across the street to this woman's house, observing the men and women jumping out of their cars to collect their food orders. Many times, I was almost enticed to go across the street and buy some food from her. However, I don't know the woman, and I'm a little skeptical about accepting food from people I don't know.

We were accusing the old woman of being a soucouyant because she looks so young and refreshed, as if she had never lifted a hand. The soucouyant is a traditional folktale from the Caribbean. According to the story, the soucouyant is a supernatural being who has made a pact with the devil to be able to change herself into all kinds of different forms. At night she sheds her human skin and changes into a ball of fire or any kind of animal. She casts spells on people to turn them into animals. She has to slip back into her human skin before dawn breaks and the cock crows, otherwise she will not be able to get back into it. When people suspect that an old woman is a soucouyant, they may trick her by going to her house at night and destroying the skin she left behind by putting salt on it so that it shrinks. She will not be able to get back into it, and thus she will die. In Trinidad, if somebody walks around with a hickey (soukie) on his neck, he may get remarks from his friends like, "Eh, Eh, Soucouyant suck yuh or wha?"

Old people say that if you wish to discover who the soucouyant in your village is, empty 100 pounds of rice at the village crossroads. She will be compelled to pick them up, one grain at a time. That is how you'll know the soucouyant.

You never see her until evening, when she goes out to the back of her house and cooks up her pot of "food" to entice people to come and eat. You should never eat the soucouyant's food, because you will keep coming back for more, and she will want something in return.

I use this folktale as an excuse for not trying her food. I relate her to the traditional folk character because I was amazed to see people on a daily basis coming to buy her food, which is something I never saw before. I also couldn't understand why I never saw the woman outside of her house, and I thought of the soucouyant, who no one sees until the evening when she flies off to find her victims. However in this case, the woman entices strangers to come to her house and buy food.

INTERVIEW WITH TISHA

My name is Tisha Andrea Peters. I used to live in Crown Heights, on New York Avenue.

How would you compare Seaview to where you lived before?
It's much different. It's quieter. No one is hanging out. It's much better, much quieter. People have different mentalities. It's beautiful. It's a nice place to raise children, that's my opinion.

What was your childhood like?
My mother kept me secluded from Crown Heights. I was from there, but she took me out of the neighborhood. I saw different things. The neighborhood was drug infested. I knew about it but still wasn't exposed to it because of the way my mother was. She wasn't like the people in the neighborhood, even though we lived there.

Thinking about your childhood and the way people behaved compared to now – do you think a lot of people are the same?

I believe it's gotten worse. The children are picking up the same behavior, mentality, and don't-value-life type attitude that the older generation had.

In the old neighborhood, Crown Heights, they're not friendly at all. Children have no respect for their elders. They don't value life. Most of them are high-school dropouts. Their parents were the same. The older people have that mentality, sitting on the stoop, not working, welfare, and things of that nature.

In Canarsie, people pretty much say hello. If you're new in a neighborhood, everyone wants to know who you are. Canarsie was all white before. The minorities moved in now, even though you still have people from the old Canarsie here. People are more family-oriented and involved in the community. Everyone sticks together.

How would you describe Canarsie – is it one of the neighborhoods that is more diverse, compared to a place like Bed-Stuy?

Now it's diverse. From, like 1992–2007, there has been a change. Now the majority of residents are Black people from different Caribbean backgrounds, African Americans, New Yorkers, and Southerners. They're the majority now. It's the changing of Canarsie.

You're kind of away from the business. Everything shuts down early here. You don't have too many stores, so you don't see traffic and people. You'll see people walking around during the day. But as soon as it gets dark, there are no children outside. No drunks. No one is on the corner playing dice or anything. It's just much different.

Even though I've been here since March of 2007, there are some people I still don't know. Because even though it's a friendly community, they come in and they come out. Everyone is going in his or her own direction. It's very weird.

Do you ever feel like you wish you had more of a connection with people in the neighborhood, or do you like it that way?

I don't want to be friendly with the whole neighborhood, just to an extent where we know each other, because the kids play together.

I noticed when you guys were living on Church and Nostrand, you would usually find somebody visiting on the weekend. Your mother was living with you guys. How did your mother's passing away affect your connection with family?

Naturally when someone passes away, we try to stick together. But in reality, everyone has his or her own life, so we kind of separated. We stay in contact as much as we can.

Where did the idea of coming to Canarsie come from?

In my wildest dreams, I never thought I would move to Canarsie because it's too quiet and I didn't really have too many family members who lived in the area. But it was the only place that was available at the time. We got a good deal. We came here to give it a try. We actually love Canarsie now. It's quiet. It just has different scenery from where I was living before.

Do you know what goes on in Seaview Park? It seems like a lot of families hang out there, sometimes during the weekend. They have these family events.

Yeah, you have camps that go out there because they have children's summer programs. They have basketball teams from the Hebrew Educational Society in Seaview. They have tournaments for different sports and for cricket. People from all over the Caribbean have different teams that play in the summer. People have barbecues and family picnics, and they play soccer.

So, do you ever feel like you need a vacation from this area or just from being in this house?

I go into the old neighborhood – Crown Heights, Flatbush – for shopping. Certain things that you would get out there, you can't get over here. First of all Canarsie is overpriced. And sometimes when it gets too quiet, I want to hear a little bit of noise.

How did you meet my brother?

I met him in detention in 1994 at Boys and Girls High School. We were friends, but then we lost contact. I thought he was a nut, so I said, "I'm not calling him; he's a jerk." But later on, we got back together and had a serious relationship. Now we have three beautiful children: Christina, nine; Isaiah, eight; and Sapphire, 10 months. So we go back a long way: 1994 to 2007.

How would you compare the '80s to now?

In the '80s you still experienced racism. If a Black person went to Howard Beach, the white people there would look at them funny and chase them out the neighborhood. I couldn't see myself living in Canarsie back in the '80s.

Do you think there are people who live in Seaview who were housekeepers and they just moved themselves up?

Oh yes, definitely. You have people with Caribbean backgrounds who own houses. They clean houses and baby-sit children until they work their way up. They get their green card, and they save their money. It's an investment for them. Not all people who own houses out here are doctors, or work for the city, or things like that. You have regular people who obtain the American dream.

Do you know anyone personally who had this experience?

I know someone in Canarsie who owns a house in Flatlands Five. She's from Jamaica. She wanted to be a nurse, but she never pursued her career. Her mother told her to go clean peoples' houses instead. She came in the '80s. She went to a career-initiative school to be a dental assistant. She went there and got certified by the state. Her first job paid $10 an hour, and now she's been doing it for 20 years. She has her own house in Flatlands Five, which is one of the most expensive areas in Canarsie. Paerdegat, Flatlands Five, and 105 around the 100s have the most expensive houses. She's been living there since the '90s. She's still a dental assistant. She makes $18 an hour, but she owns a house. So she saved her money, and she also has tenants in her house.

It's a smart move. Do you think you'll continue to stay in Canarsie?

I'm just taking it one day at a time. If I'm in the position to get my own house, I'll do that. Maybe in Canarsie, maybe not. I don't know yet.

So what is one of your dreams in life?

I'd like to get to the point where my kids are OK. Everyone wants to be financially stable. Not to buy a Mercedes Benz or a house in the Hamptons, but just to set up your kids so they won't have the same struggles. I want to try to make the best of it and to instill values in them, which most kids don't have these days.

My thing is to get a degree in nursing or biology. I'd like to travel. I've been to different places. I wish I could move to St. Martins. I just want to call an agency and say, "Book me a flight to such and such for seven days and eight nights." I don't really ask for too much.

A NIGHT OF INTRUSION

One Sunday evening, I left my brother's house really late because I was intoxicated with a good Sunday dinner and kept extending the minute that I would leave. I kept saying to myself, "Five more minutes!" Then it was around nine o'clock, which was the time when buses stop running frequently in Canarsie. So my brother, Mohammed, insisted on walking me to the bus stop. As we were walking, we came across a man who was arguing with a woman about money. My brother and I assumed that it was the usual "baby mama drama" episode until my brother noticed another woman sitting in the car seat with her skirt up. The other woman standing outside of the car was barely dressed. They looked like three musketeers, caught in a lustful rumble. The mystery man's face was flustered, as if he was just caught red-handed, though he was dressed in the very best preppy attire and was flaunting a golden Rolex.

Anyway, my brother thought the man was prostituting them, and so did the neighbor who called the police. Suddenly, two police cars drove up to the corner of the block and began to question the trio. I was shocked at how fast the cops appeared. People there always complain about the police never coming unless someone suspects drug- and gang-related activities going on. My brother laughed saying, "You can't have that go down in Canarsie, especially not in front of someone's house. Someone called the police." In my mind, I pictured an old woman in a pink slip whispering into the phone to the police and peeping out of the window to see if the people were still here. She probably said to herself, "Jesus, look at this man and these girls. I can't believe they have all this on display. Do they know that it's Sunday?"

The cops told the man to leave, and he soon gathered himself with his woman in the fancy SUV and spun off. The other woman called up her friend to pick her up, while trying not to explain how she was dismissed by her sugar daddy.

I found this whole situation hilarious because while all of this was going on, there was a "Trini Family and Friends" event taking place in the park: a friendly outing for all Trinidadian families. This event is for Trinidadians only. However, the organizers welcome anyone who is willing to buy red t-shirts labeled "Trini Family and Friends." So you saw many parents and their kids trying to avoid the disruptive behavior while leaving the park. One of the children asked his parents, "Mommy, why are the cops here?" The woman ignored her son's question by asking him what he wanted for a snack. My brother and I could not stop laughing.

As the bus approached, two old ladies appeared out of nowhere. They were so eager to get on the bus that they pushed right past us. Of course, they're supposed to go first because they're senior citizens. So, as usual, I chose to sit in the front of the bus and gaze at the beautiful green landscapes. Everyone on the bus was so quiet and well mannered, as if they were under surveillance – everyone except a Haitian man, who began to fuss. He wanted to stand beside the bus driver, even though he knew that passengers must stand behind the yellow line. So when the bus driver gave him a very stern look, he knew that it was only going to cause trouble. The man swiftly went to the back of the bus while cursing like a drunken sailor. However, no one paid him any attention, except me, who enjoys being the spectator.

Or could it be possible that I am an intruder, because I am not a resident of Seaview? I don't go to "Trini Family and Friends" shindigs, I'm not provoked to call the cops by watching slackness, and I prefer to leave the bus drivers alone. (Don't be fooled by the MTA badge; you never know when they might snap.) But I am drawn to Seaview because of its peaceful atmosphere and remoteness from urban New York.

» ABOUT THE NYC NEIGHBORHOOD STORY PROJECT «

In June 2005, just before Hurricane Katrina, I read a series of books written by high school students from New Orleans, documenting the unique and vibrant culture of many of that city's neighborhoods. Even though I'd never been to New Orleans, after reading the books, I felt like I knew the city's people and neighborhoods. So rarely are the real voices of real people presented so clearly, without appropriation. Everyone's story is presented with respect and dignity. The work felt so closely aligned with what we do at NY Writers Coalition, that I immediately thought, "We must do this in New York City."

More than three years later, we are thrilled to present the book you just read, the first by the NYC Neighborhood Story Project. Much happened in the past few years to make this book possible, and thanks are due to so many people for their encouragement, support and tireless work.

First of all, to all the writers for pushing themselves to the limits and producing amazing work. Also, to their friends, family and neighbors who shared their stories.

To Project Director/Editor Kesha Young, who joined this project beyond midstream and lovingly brought her incredible creativity to every task, big or small.

To the Urban Academy community, for their support of the project. And to teachers Caitlin Schlapp-Gitloff and Becky Walzer for brilliance, patience, innovation and countless hours of hard work.

To Rachel Breunlin and Abram Himelstein of the Neighborhood Story Project, for trusting us with their brainchild, and for endless amounts of insight, guidance and inspiration.

To Johnny Temple and Johanna Ingalls of Akashic Books, for holding our hands through every step of the book-publishing process.

To Sohrab Habibon for his brilliant cover design and book layout. To photographers Elissa Benes and Jason Gardner for adding their beautiful images to the book.

To StoryCorps, for guidance and facilitation. To Dave Isay, for his inspiration and time. To Sophie McManus and Kesha Young for facilitating creative writing workshops.

To the reading committee, Jamie Shearn Coan, Michele Gilliam, Raina Wallens, Nancy Weber and Betty Lou Young for their invaluable feedback on the manuscript. To Tamiko Beyer for her copyediting prowess. And again to Michele Gilliam for transcribing hours of interviews, and to Barbara Schlapp and the volunteers who transcribed the rest of the interviews.

To our funders, Time Warner's Youth Media and Arts Fund, the Hot Topic Foundation, the Independence Community Foundation, the Kalliopeia Foundation, the Pinkerton Foundation, the Union Square Arts Awards, Valentine Perry Snyder Fund, the NYC Department of Cultural Affairs, the NY State Council For The Arts, NY State Senator Velmanette Montgomery, The Mary Duke Biddle Foundation, and all our individual donors for their generous support.

Aaron Zimmerman
Executive Director, NY Writers Coalition

»ABOUT NEW YORK WRITERS COALITION (NYWC)«

NYWC, a 501(c)3 not-for-profit organization creates opportunities for formerly voiceless members of society to be heard through the art of writing. We provide free, unique, and powerful creative-writing workshops throughout New York City for people from groups that have been historically deprived of voice in our society, including at-risk youth, adult residents of supportive housing, the formerly incarcerated, seniors, and others.

NYWC is one of the largest community-based writing organizations in the country. Each year, we conduct more than one thousand workshop sessions at approximately 45 locations, creating ongoing writing communities throughout the city. We've published two book-length anthologies of writing by our workshop members: *The Hidden Chorus* and *If These Streets Could Talk*, and numerous smaller chapbooks of our writers' work. We also publish *Plum Biscuit*, an online literary magazine edited by our workshop members.

NYWC also operates the **Writing Aloud** reading series, a monthly event featuring members of our workshops reading alongside established authors; **Write Makes Might**, an annual marathon reading by our workshop members; and is a partner in the annual **Fort Greene**

Park Summer Literary Festival, a series of writing workshops for young people culminating in a reading by the young writers with literary icons such as Amiri Baraka, Jhumpa Lahiri, Sonia Sanchez, and Sapphire. Workshop participants have had poems, stories, and plays published and performed. Others have read their writing on NPR's *All Things Considered*, WNYC's *Brian Lehrer Show* and WBAI's *Global Movements, Urban Struggles*.

To find out more, including how you can support us by becoming a member or participating in our annual Write-A-Thon, please visit **www.nywriterscoalition.org**.